T0325371

The Philosophy of Wine

The Philosophy of Wine

A Case of Truth, Beauty and Intoxication

Cain Todd

McGill-Queen's University Press

Montreal & Kingston • Ithaca

© Cain Todd 2010

ISBN: 978-0-7735-3838-2

Legal deposit fourth quarter 2010
Bibliothèque nationale du Québec

Published simultaneously outside North America
by Acumen Publishing Limited

McGill-Queen's University Press acknowledges the financial support
of the Government of Canada through the Canada Book Fund for our
publishing activities.

Library and Archives Canada Cataloguing in Publication

Todd, Cain Samuel, 1976–
    The philosophy of wine : a case of truth, beauty, and intoxication /
Cain Samuel Todd.

Includes bibliographical references and index.
ISBN 978-0-7735-3838-2

    1. Wine--Philosophy. 2. Aesthetics. I. Title.

GT2885.T63 2011   641.2'201   C2010-906332-5

Typeset in Bembo.
Printed in the UK by the MPG Books Group.

For David & Angharad,
and my parents

Contents

Acknowledgements

Since first developing a serious interest in wine many years ago I have wanted to write something of philosophical substance about it, but I was perhaps slightly wary of devoting time to what I thought would be perceived as a frivolous topic. In addition, I was genuinely sceptical about my ability to capture in the crisp, clean and often austere language of analytic philosophy such a sensual domain of experiential value. It was only the recent burgeoning of work in this area, and the invitation from Acumen, that propelled me into action. I must therefore express my deep gratitude to my publisher, Steven Gerrard, for asking me to write this book, for his patience with the inevitable delays and for his general encouragement. I am equally indebted to Roger Scruton and Jack Bender for reading the manuscript and for their positive and critical comments. They themselves have both written with remarkable insight and understanding about the central themes of this book, so it has been immeasurably improved as a result, even if I have myself failed to make all of the changes that they suggested. I did, however, make almost all of the changes suggested by Acumen's excellent reader Kate Williams, whose impressive diligence rescued the manuscript from many errors.

Parts of this book have been presented in different versions at various conferences and workshops and I would like to thank audiences at the universities of Durham, Lancaster, Geneva, Cardiff and Rennes for their extremely useful questions and feedback. In particular, I would like to thank Barry Smith for engaging discussion on many of these issues and for the opportunity of drawing on his vast store of wine knowledge.

Finally, a few wine-oriented notes of thanks. The Cambridge University Blind Tasting Society was an excellent place to learn about wine and my only regret is having lost (twice) to Oxford in the varsity match. Long may the society continue and I am very grateful to all my fellow tasters there, in particular to Victor Chua who helped support this hedonistic hobby through a period of penury. I owe an immense debt of gratitude to all my wine-drinking friends for affording me the opportunity to drink good wine with them, and for indulging my annoying analytical drinking habits. My biggest debt, however, is reserved for David and Angharad McAlpine, who possess an astoundingly good cellar and boundless generosity, and to whom I owe all my greatest experiences of intoxication. Lastly, I must thank Alix Cohen, for not only sharing these experiences but making them all the more intoxicating.

Introduction

Does this Bonnes Mares really have notes of chocolate, truffle and *merde de cheval*? Can Chablis really possess bracing acidity and a middle palate of steely minerality reminiscent of wet stones? Assuming that winemakers in the Loire or Barossa valleys are not experimenting with some unusual ingredients, can Sancerre really smell of cat's pee or Shiraz of sweaty saddles? Can wines really be brooding, profound, elegant, pretentious, charming, cheeky or deceitful? At what point do metaphorical characterizations of wine transgress the hazy boundary dividing the imaginative and informative from the outlandish and absurd? Is Château L'Eglise Clinet 1989 really a better wine than Château Belair 1989? Can wines be expressive? Should great wines be thought of as works of art? Are there genuine experts in taste or merely pretentious snobs overburdened with the desire to dazzle and to cultivate a coterie of exclusivity and luxury masquerading under a cloak of objective quality?

These kinds of questions must at some point have entered the mind of anybody who has read a wine label, puzzled over the tasting notes of a wine writer, been baffled by the response of a sommelier to an innocent question, or participated in or simply overheard the chatter of those who, from perspectives encompassing the awed, the charitable, the sceptical and the downright scornful, might be labelled alternatively wine bores, snobs, lovers, experts or connoisseurs. If you count yourself among the puzzled, or simply wish to explore these issues in greater depth, then this book is for you. My aim is to provide a clear and engaging discussion of the philosophical significance of wine that will be accessible to all wine lovers, specialists and non-specialists, philosophers and non-philosophers, alike.

It may not have occurred even to the serious drinker that these questions are at least partly philosophical in nature. This is not surprising, for hitherto even the serious thinker – the academic philosopher – has remained largely oblivious of, indifferent to or even openly hostile towards the philosophical interest and significance of tastes, smells and wine. Indeed, it might seem odd, and perhaps even somewhat frivolous, to devote serious philosophical attention to an object that is primarily a source of sensual pleasure. It did not seem odd to the ancient Greek philosophers and tragedians, however, who extolled the virtues of wine in liberating social intercourse, lubricating intellectual thought and facilitating the unification of the good, the beautiful and the true.

Very recently there has been a flowering of interest among philosophers, but also psychologists and others, in the nature of our perception and appreciation of tastes and smells and in the pre-eminent complex human artefact constituted of them, wine. They have become aware that wine raises in particularly complex, significant and striking ways a panoply of important philosophical issues, concerning notions such as objectivity and subjectivity, the nature and epistemological status of sense perception and experience, the role of metaphor in judgement, aesthetic and artistic value, and intoxication, to mention just the most obvious.

Indeed, it would not be too much of an exaggeration to declare that wine is currently something of a hot philosophical topic. In 2007 a collection of papers on the philosophy of wine was published in the book *Questions of Taste: The Philosophy of Wine*, and this was followed in 2008 by a further collection in *Wine and Philosophy: A Symposium on Thinking and Drinking*. Then, in 2009, Roger Scruton published his *I Drink Therefore I Am: A Philosopher's Guide to Wine*. Outside the confines of academia, philosophical questions about wine have recently been pondered in the films *Sideways* (2004) and *Mondovino* (2004), and as I write this introduction the *Guardian* newspaper has housed a debate about the role and status of wine critics, which is worth dwelling on for a moment as a good indication of the ways in which philosophical issues about wine arise in non-philosophical contexts.

In a column headed "Wine Critics' Advice is Unchallenged Bunk", the *Guardian* reports that the wine expert Tim Hanni has argued that everybody has an individual taste profile, that everyone's palate is different, and hence that the advice of wine critics is irrelevant because "Taking advice from someone with a markedly different palate can be like 'trying to put on a shoe that doesn't fit'". He has, accordingly, designed a questionnaire called the "budometer" which aims to suggest to consumers wines that match their tastes. He says:

> What we have today is real chaos … The style of cabernet, for example, has changed enormously in recent years, and "experts" now write entirely competing views on it. Received wisdom holds that certain wines are simply the best, and that anyone who disagrees is stupid, unsophisticated, or both. That's more chaotic than giving people the confidence to drink what they like, no matter what the bottle costs, and no matter what food they enjoy it with.[1]

A few days after this column was published, Tim Atkin wrote a response entitled "Why Wine Critics are Useful" in the same newspaper. Rejecting the charge of snobbery as unjust, he writes:

> I'd be the first to agree with Tim Hanni that everyone's palate is different. But I also think that wine tasting is something you need to practise. Some people are innately brilliant at assessing wine, but most of us have to work at it to acquire reliable, trustworthy palates. You wouldn't expect someone who's been playing the piano for a year

---

1. Reported in www.guardian.co.uk/lifeandstyle/2010/feb/04/wine-critics-advice-unchallenged- bunk (accessed September 2010).

to tackle a Chopin Prelude, so why should wine be different? Professionals are invariably better at tasting because
it's their full-time job. Do I believe that you should follow
your own judgement? Of course I do ... People who buy
wines they don't like because someone else tells them to
are fools. This doesn't undermine the role of the critic,
however. Just as I read Philip French on film and Michael
Billington on theatre, so I would advise you to find a wine
critic, or set of critics, whose judgement you trust ...[2]

Who is right? Much of the book shall be preoccupied with this
and similar questions, and the tenor of this debate serves to highlight
some of the confusion that afflicts lay discussions of these issues. It
is the philosopher's job to disentangle and analyse them. To pre-
empt a little, we can see that both writers are in some way right.
Individual preferences for different tastes, types and styles of wine
may indeed be subjective, without this rather trivial fact impugning
the objectivity of judgements about the characteristics of wines.
Whether a wine has crisp acidity and an aroma of cut grass is one
thing, whether this is to your taste is quite another. Expert critics
may be able to help you determine the former without thereby
offering criticisms of the latter. Although, as we shall see, evaluations of wine quality introduce a great deal of complexity into
these considerations, whatever the chain of association in the minds

---

2. www.guardian.co.uk/lifeandstyle/wordofmouth/2010/feb/09/wine-
criticism (accessed September 2010).

of some people that equates wine critics with snobbery, there is clearly no inevitable route from the one to the other; as, indeed, Atkin's own view reveals. Snobbery is a type of attitude, expertise a capacity to know and to judge accurately or appropriately.

Unfortunately, confusion is rife in popular discussions of wine expertise, appreciation and evaluation, partly because even the best wine experts themselves do not always discuss these issues with sufficient philosophical clarity and perspicuity. The well-known wine writer Jancis Robinson, for example, is far from atypical in claiming, on the one hand, that wine tasting is the "definitive subjective sport", in which there are "no absolutes … so the opinion of the novice is every bit as valuable as that of the expert" (2003: 18), while on the other hand participating fully in all those practices integral to the wine world that presuppose the existence of expertise and certain objective norms: making judgements about wine character, advising buyers and producers, endorsing ranking systems and giving value scores out of twenty or one hundred, and arguing with other critics. Hugh Johnson, too, writes that "The wine trade has interests in convincing you and me that quality is something objective and measurable. You and I know that it is no such thing: you love what you love" (in Beckett 2008: 6). In admirable haste to discharge accusations of elitism, obfuscation and snobbery, critics frequently lurch into proclamations of subjectivity that are directly at odds with their own implicit beliefs and explicit practices.

There are, happily, ways of reconciling these apparent tensions, clearing up confusions, charitably interpreting such statements and championing the objectivity and seriousness of our appreciation of wine, which I, as a non-expert, hope to do in writing this book. Inevitably, my motivations are largely personal. I learned about wine through joining a blind tasting society while a graduate student, an experience that was revelatory. The journey that begins from an impressive lack of knowledge, understanding and experience – and an inability to distinguish two white wines from one another, let alone use any meaningful words to describe them – and leads to the gradual development of an ability to interpret and appreciate the complexity and unique values of an object that, at first, is just an alcoholic drink, is quite incredible.

Through this experience, and the subsequent largesse of generous friends, I have been fortunate to have tasted some of the world's great wines and it is simply true that they can open one's eyes, mind and palate to a world of values of which one was hitherto completely oblivious. Drinking them is the best, and I think probably the only foolproof way of responding adequately to those who are wary or contemptuous of the world of wine. These are intensely personal experiences that cannot be reported or captured entirely in words, any more than great works of music or art can be so captured. One needs to drink for oneself. Sadly, like the situation prevailing in the world of art, the world's best wines sell for ludicrous prices and are now all but unaffordable for most people. This is not only a great shame from an aesthetic point of view, but to my mind something approaching a moral outrage, for not to be able to try such wines, or to be able to appreciate them, is to be deprived of values that are,

I believe, worth experiencing for their own sake, and without which the world would be a poorer place. Just how much poorer is, of course, a tricky question, and one we shall alight on later in the book.

It is no surprise that the scepticism about the value and interest of wine that has hitherto prevailed, more or less since ancient Greece, has gone hand in hand with a thorough neglect of, and in some religiously inspired strands of thought active contempt for, the senses of taste and smell, and their relegation to the margins of philosophical and scientific interest. This, as I noted above, is now rapidly changing, and a significant number of contemporary philosophers have defended the objectivity of our judgements concerning wine and waxed lyrical about its intrinsic and instrumental values. And these too will form the key themes that dominate my discussion as I try throughout to distil these views while offering in addition my own sustained defence of the objectivity of wine judgements, a demystification and defence of the nature of expertise, and a theory of the aesthetic value of wine and its appreciation.

In spite of the welcome sympathy with which wine is now viewed by many, however, I do not think that philosophers have yet succeeded in fathoming the depths of the rich and assorted values inherent in wine, values that in my view reveal important insights about ourselves, our multifarious interests and pleasures, the nature of appreciation, and the meaningfulness and emotional expressivity that objects in the world can attain for us. I hope this book goes some way towards revealing these.

A note on the text and terminology

For the sake of ease and clarity, I have endeavoured to keep notes, references and philosophical jargon to a minimum throughout. I have also tried to keep to a minimum the level of philosophical background presupposed. Nonetheless, some of the discussion is inevitably a little technical, and the non-specialist may find some parts of Chapters 3 and 4, and the final section of Chapter 5 a little challenging.

A quick point of terminology: I am careful throughout to distinguish the aromas, smells or bouquet of wine from its tastes, where the former refer to the properties discerned by our sense of smell, and the latter refers to our sense of taste. However, I will also sometimes refer to the overall *taste* (or sometimes *flavour*) of the wine where this clearly means the overall sensory experience of it, including its aromas and felt textures in addition to its literal tastes. The context of the discussion will always make it clear what "taste" is being used to refer to.

1

The Experience of Wine

Tasting, Smelling and Knowing

Common-sense doubts

Philosophical reflection on the nature of wine, our experience of it and pleasure in drinking it has been firmly rooted in the ordinary, everyday observation that, in the hierarchy of importance, our senses of taste and smell seem to lie well below vision, hearing and touch. By "importance" I do not just mean basic survival value, for although we can survive without sight and hearing, and (perhaps with more difficulty) touch, our full engagement with the complex social and cultural world so vital to human flourishing depends on the pre-eminence of these senses. In contrast, although our senses of smell and taste can bring us pleasure, and in certain cases alert us to potential dangers, they can seem much less vital to our existence and well-being, and the pleasures they provide of far less interest and consequence than the objects we contemplate in sight and sound. Hence the scepticism frequently directed, for example, at claims that there can be objective standards of taste, or that food and drink can be genuine or serious objects of aesthetic interest, claims that we shall examine in some detail later.

These purported differences between the different senses and their objects are reflected in the apparent fact that we are, in general, simply much less good at smelling and tasting than we are at seeing, hearing and touching. It is often claimed that we can detect, identify and discriminate a substantially more limited range of tastes and odours than we can colours and sounds, for example. Scientific research appears to confirm this, demonstrating that whereas we are able to see millions of different colours, we can smell merely thousands of different odorants or volatile compounds (between 10,000 and 100,000) and although there is some dispute about the exact number of tastes, these are generally limited to sourness, bitterness, sweetness, saltiness and umami. I shall return to the empirical research on taste and smell below.

But the contrast is not merely quantitative; it is also qualitative. Our taste and smell perception seem less finely tuned, less able to discern the subtle differences between various sensations in our mouths and noses, especially when confronted with complex medleys of tastes and smells – such as we find in wines and perfumes – which all too readily become blended and jumbled together. We easily confuse tastes and smells, and our very ability to detect them seems fragile and fallible, as befits the ephemeral and ethereal quality of the elusive chemical "objects" of our sense perception, which are liable to fade and vanish quickly, and to be easily affected and masked by other tastes and smells. A slight cold can strongly and adversely affect our ability to detect tastes and odours, and you would be well advised not to brush your teeth, drink coffee or eat a spicy curry before a wine tasting.

One needs also to be aware of the ease with which our taste and smell perceptions are influenced by suggestion. Any wine taster will have experienced, at one time or another, their hesitant identification of wine aromas being instantly and irreversibly affected by the loud pronouncements of a more confident voice at the table. This phenomenon goes hand in hand with a common "tip of the tongue" affliction when confronted with even quite familiar smells and tastes, and we frequently struggle to remember and re-identify even the relatively simple mixtures of aromas in not-so-fine wines. How clearly can you remember all the flavours you detected in the last bottle of wine you consumed? This all contrasts quite starkly with the certainty and clarity with which we seem to detect, describe and remember the objects of sight, sound and touch in our environment.

This impoverished status of taste and smell in our perceptual engagement with, and understanding of, the world around us is further clearly reflected, so it has been claimed, in the impoverished vocabulary we have to describe tastes and smells, and our remarkably poor ability to capture our experiences of them in words. We are generally reduced to naming tastes and smells in terms of the substances that reliably cause them, or of which we are reminded – for example, lemony, woody, smoky, and so on – but naming the substances that have tastes and smells is not the same thing as naming or describing the taste or smell itself.

And when it comes to describing new and complex aromas, and mixtures of aromas, such as those found in perfumes and wines, we are generally at a loss to know what to say, as any beginner on a wine tasting course can readily testify.

For all of these reasons we trust our taste and smell perceptions and memories less than our visual, auditory and tactile perceptions and memories, and we are wary of sharing and comparing our gustatory experiences. When faced with apparent disagreement over descriptions and evaluations of food and drink we are often inclined to shrug our shoulders and withdraw to the diffident claim "it's just a matter of taste", implying that there is really nothing to disagree about, no fact, no truth of the matter. One person's sweet is another's bitter, but one person's square is not another's circle, and anybody with a minimal ear for music can hear when a singer is out of tune. To introduce a philosophically loaded – and, as we shall see later, extremely slippery – term, tastes and smells appear, for all of these reasons, to be purely *subjective*; hence the common phrase "*De gustibus non est disputandum*": "there is no disputing about taste".

It should thus be no surprise that these sceptical tendencies surface in yet stronger forms when confronted with the great variety and complexity of tastes and smells that constitute wine, and with the panoply of often baffling social, economic, cultural, linguistic and technological phenomena that surround its production, consumption and appreciation. Mild scepticism may then even blossom into open contempt for what is perceived to be a fraudulent, deceptive, pretentious and elitist façade of expertise and objectivity plastered thinly over mere subjective taste: taste, moreover, that is concerned with objects that simply cannot bear the weight of the complex metaphorical descriptions and evaluations heaped upon them by supposed experts.

How could a mere mixture of chemical odorants, however complex, be accurately or appropriately described as feminine or pretentious? How could it even be meaningful to describe one mixture of smells as "better" than another, unless all that means is that somebody happens to prefer that mixture to the other, that it gives them more sensual enjoyment?

Hopefully this way of putting the matter will seem relatively intuitive and familiar, and common-sense doubts have been echoed in many respects by philosophical reflection. By adding more detailed thoughts and arguments, and some judicious sprinkling of recent evidence from psychology and neuroscience, some philosophers have reached similarly negative conclusions about the status of these neglected senses and the objects constituted by them. "Neglected" here is worth emphasizing, for as I noted in the Introduction, until relatively recently philosophers – and to a lesser, but by no means inconsiderable extent, psychologists, chemists and neuroscientists – have devoted remarkably little attention to taste and smell. Although some interesting historical, cultural and religious reasons can be adduced to explain in part this neglect, these need not detain us now. So let's turn to the philosophical arguments before examining the relevant empirical data.

Philosophical scepticism

The common-sense intuitions and suspicions just presented have been formulated and defended philosophically by appealing to the metaphysical and epistemological status of tastes and smells,[1] and in particular by the privileging of sight as the model for understanding all sense perception.

Philosophers talk about perception being "representational". That is, when we see the wine bottle in front of us on the table we have a perceptual visual experience that represents the wine bottle. The history of philosophy is awash with disputes about the nature of this representation, particularly with the question of whether it is a thing in the head that we perceive – the "image" of the wine bottle – or whether we directly perceive the "real" wine bottle that exists externally, out there in the world, independently of us and our experiences of it. Mercifully, we can remain relatively aloof from these disputes and focus instead on the idea that visual and auditory perception seem to give us direct access to the world in a way that taste and smell perception do not.

If I smell what seems to be food burning in the kitchen I may infer from my experience that food is burning in the kitchen, but of course I might be wrong about this for I could just be smelling the lingering odour of this burning, which is no longer hap-

---

1. "Metaphysical" here simply refers to what there is in the world, to whether something exists. "Epistemological" means having to do with knowledge and our ability to know about things in the world.

pening. So my judgement "the food is burning" will in that case be mistaken. The smell was, as it were, only in the head (or the nose). In contrast, if I see the food burning I do not need to make an inference that the food is burning: I simply see that it is. Of course, I can make errors in visual perception, as when I mistake a person for somebody else, or when I see a straight stick in water as bent, but the point is that vision has a certain directness in its relation to the world it represents, which smell and taste seem to lack. Vision, philosophers are wont to say, is essentially *veridical*; it gets the world right.

Philosophers sometimes characterize this difference by applying the label "distal senses" to sight and hearing, and emphasizing in contrast the chemical nature of our "gustatory senses" of taste and smell, which require a penetration of, and interaction with, our bodies. In visual and auditory representations, it is sometimes claimed, I *see through* or *hear through* the perceptual experience *to* the objects that are the causes of these experiences, whereas taste and smell seem to represent nothing beyond the experiences of taste and smell in our own bodies.

Here is an example of this type of claim from Roger Scruton, who argues that, unlike the sense of sight, taste and smell "do not represent a world independent of themselves". He says that "visual experience reaches through the 'look' of a thing to the thing that looks. I don't 'sniff through' the smell to the thing that smells, for the thing is not represented in its smell in the way that it is represented in its visual appearance" (2007: 4–5).

So, the claim is that the world represented in visual perception is represented to us *as* a world of separate, independent objects, and the various features of those objects are represented as being the real properties of those objects. The blueness of the cushion is in the cushion; it is not in me, and moreover it seems to us that this is the case *in our perception*. In contrast, when we smell something, the smell seems to be located in us, in our nose or in our minds, and not in the world in the way that the visual blueness of the cushion seems to be an objective part of the cushion.

In fact, these differences are actually quite difficult to make precise, and it is not obvious that in these respects sounds resemble sights more than tastes and smells. But some philosophers have also contended that our visual and auditory perceptions are informationally richer than our taste and smell perceptions. Whereas sounds have dimensions of pitch, timbre and volume, and colours possess hue, saturation and brightness, it seems that tastes and odours vary only in intensity. This relative simplicity helps explain the marked quantitative and qualitative poverty of the vocabulary we can call on to describe tastes and smells, and our difficulty in capturing our experiences of them in words; they simply lack the dimensional richness and complexity required to do so.

A further, related claim often made is that the information provided by vision and audition is, or can be, spatially and temporally ordered and structured in ways that reflect the nature of the objects perceived, which is beyond the power of taste and smell to represent. Thus, for example, vision allows us to determine the various dimensions of physical objects, offering us multiple perspectives that enable us to determine an object's identity, while we can hear sounds as temporally successive and bearing certain relations to each other that we characterize, for example, as higher or lower. This is what allows sounds to be ordered as they are in the "movement" we hear in music. In contrast, it has been claimed, smells and tastes intermingle in ways that exhibit no real order or structure. As William Lycan puts it:

> a smell seems a modification of our own consciousness rather than a stable property of a perceptual object that would exist unperceived ... Vision ... offers a multitude of different perspectives that are, to some extent, under the subject's control ... [In contrast we] cannot easily see how one could *entirely by smell* check and recheck an external object's identity or character by gaining successively different olfactory perspectives on that object.
>
> (2000: 277)

The *metaphysical* upshot of these considerations appears to be this: smells and tastes – that is, as "objects", the things we sense through our taste and smell perceptions in the nose and mouth – are not genuine properties of the objects that are their source, and our experiences of them do not genuinely represent their objects. Rather, they are essentially properties of our experiences. They are subjective rather than objective kinds of things. In this respect they are more like pains and itches than genuine perceptions.

More precisely, tastes and smells are what philosophers sometimes refer to as *secondary qualities*. *Primary qualities*, such as shape, weight and texture, are held to properly belong to physical objects independently of us; we detect them primarily by sight and touch, and we perceive them *as* so belonging. In contrast, secondary qualities depend on our subjective impressions of objects and are thus sometimes labelled *response-dependent* properties. They spring into existence only through our interaction with the world and hence do not correspond to the way things really are independently of how we experience them. The lemon is not *really* bitter: the bitterness is simply a property of how we taste it and belongs to our experience and not to the lemon.

The *epistemological* implication is that our smell and taste perceptions give us no *cognitive* access to the world; we cannot get genuine knowledge about objects from merely tasting and smelling. It seems to follow straightforwardly that our judgements about taste and smell lack any claim to objective validity. You cannot, as it were, be in error about what you smell, although you might of course be in error about the nature of the object you attribute it to. Why? Because there is no objective correlate to your smell or taste in the object *independently of you*. One person's bitter may indeed be another's sweet.

These claims also have implications for views about the *aesthetic* value of tastes and smells, which we shall explore later, but for the moment we need to consider what all of this has to do with wine. Given that our appreciation of wine is of an object primarily constituted by tastes and smells, the claims of philosophers outlined above are straightforwardly applicable to it. If tastes and smells are subjective and non-representational in the ways suggested, when we attempt to describe and evaluate wine via these tastes and smells there is reason to think we are not really describing the *real way* the wine is at all. Rather, what I am describing is merely my own taste and smell experience, and such an experience is a necessarily subjective, private affair that can make no claim on how others do or should experience a particular wine.

So, there seems to be no question of whether the Condrieu *really* smells of ripe apricots and honey, or whether the Barbaresco *really* possesses a voluptuous body with hints of violet and raspberries framed by firm but well-integrated tannins. These are merely descriptions of my own taste and smell experiences. Thus, we seem forced to conclude, when appreciating wine we are not really appreciating or describing an independent "wine object", but merely a range of subjective experiences somehow occasioned by it. Thus, it also seems to follow that there is no point at all to wine criticism, and no real role for "expertise", other perhaps than to indulge a propensity for elaborate verbal play.

Indeed, one might draw a yet starker sceptical conclusion from these metaphysical and epistemological observations: there simply is no such object as *the real wine*. This view represents a stronger, more radically subjective view of the nature of our appreciation of wine, for it claims that the glass before us contains merely a bundle of volatile chemical compounds, constantly interacting and changing, and becoming a determinate *thing* only on their ingestion by a sniffing and swallowing subject. But in that case, it seems, there will be as many wine objects as there are such encounters. There is no such thing as *the* wine that is the object of our experiences, only the experiences occasioned by the stuff in the glass, and the most that can be said about that stuff is that it is the source of the tastes and smells that we experience.

Well, it looks now as though we have arrived at an extremely counter-intuitive position from which no obvious path leads us into illumination. The wine object either does not as such exist, or at best remains mysterious and unknowable, and any attempt to describe and evaluate it will be like trying to look at it through a glass darkly. It is important to note, however, that this view will be damaging to the notions of expertise and objectivity only in so far as it presupposes that the experiences to which wine gives rise are all different and cannot be compared. But why should we accept this? After all, don't wine experts, in virtue of their shared extensive knowledge, training and experience, thereby share the same experiences of wine? And doesn't wine expertise consist precisely in enabling us to discern how a wine *really* tastes, apart from our impoverished and idiosyncratic individual subjective reactions?

At this point it is usual to point both to the purportedly high level of disagreements even among supposed experts, as well as to a range of scientific tests and experiments that are frequently taken to demonstrate that expertise is all smoke and mirrors, with a healthy dose of bluff thrown in for good measure. Before examining the empirical data ourselves, however, it is important to turn briefly to a serious challenge to expertise and objectivity recently delivered by the philosopher Kent Bach and which has a not insignificant bearing on how we interpret this data.

Bach himself turns to science, which, he says, demonstrates that our ability to detect a vast array of many thousands of odour compounds is simply natural, innate and unlearned just as it is in the case of colour perception. In light of this, he considers whether the background knowledge, experience, training and a developed professional vocabulary on which expertise is founded can affect (a) one's pleasure in tasting wine, and (b) one's ability to detect and discriminate tastes and smells in wine.

He gives a resounding "no" to both claims, and holds that when an expert points out the distinctive qualities in a wine, she is not *revealing* qualities you hadn't noticed, but "merely calling them to your attention under a certain apt description". That is, knowledge can help us *notice* qualities, and pay attention to them, but not *uncover* them, because they were there being sensed by us all along. Moreover, he claims, the wine does not "taste different now that its qualities are singled out and labelled"; rather, "the description ring[s] true because it captures the experience one was already having" (2007: 37).

Now, this account depends on making a sharp distinction between sensation and cognition, and the pleasures and experiences proper to each. Sensory pleasures are simply those that we receive from anything that stimulates our five senses, including the pleasures of eating and drinking things that taste, smell, look, feel or sound nice. Cognitive pleasures, however, as the name suggests, are those we get from knowing certain things – such as being able to name all the Burgundy *grands crus* – and from exercising our intellectual capacities, such as when thinking philosophically about wine. Bach is arguing that while knowledge about wine is valuable in helping one know what to drink, and in being able to provide cognitive or intellectual pleasure while drinking, it can never actually enhance the sensory pleasures in drinking wine, nor enhance our ability to detect and discriminate tastes and smells. Why? Because he holds that our perception of taste and smell is, to use a piece of philosophical jargon, *cognitively impenetrable*.

Recall the example I used earlier of *seeing* a stick in water *as* bent that one *knows* really to be straight. What we know does not affect what we see. Similarly, in the case of wine what we know does not affect what we taste; our perception is thus not penetrated by cognition. Bach also makes an important contrast with our aesthetic appreciation of artworks in this respect, one that will be important to keep in mind for our later discussion. Our aesthetic appreciation of art, he suggests, is affected by knowledge, which "leads to aesthetic appreciation by enhancing one's ability to notice features and relationships that would otherwise escape one's attention" (2007: 33). But no such knowledge is required for appreciating wine, he claims, for unlike art "One doesn't have to discern complex formal or structural features and relationships, for which sustained and repeated encounters are likely to be required. No interpretation or understanding is needed" (33–4).

In short, if Bach is right then expertise is valuable only in increasing our knowledge about wine, and our enjoyment in conversing knowledgably about it, but it has no significant impact on our sensory experience of wine, which is just a matter of subjective taste. As such, the practices of explanation, evaluation and understanding presupposed by wine criticism appear to be directly threatened.

Happily, Bach is not right, as anybody with any experience of blind tasting will, with a little reflection, be able to point out. Before exploring this further, we should turn now to some of the empirical studies of wine and its appreciation in order to see whether they cast any light on the philosophical claims we have been exploring, and whether they support these sceptical views.

Science and subjectivity

First, we need some basic understanding of how smell and taste perception work, but it is important to note that this is a very complex area and that, despite the recent marked increase in research activity and interest, the science of olfaction is in many respects still in its infancy. Thus, many central aspects of our taste and smell perception and processing, as well as our knowledge of the immense number of molecular compounds, chemical processes and interactions in wine, remain unclear and the subject of ongoing investigation. One must be especially wary, therefore, of drawing philosophical conclusions from the empirical data in this area. Thankfully, a number of wine writers have brought to light much of this research and presented it in a clear and accessible form. The *locus classicus* here is Émile Peynaud's

The Taste of Wine: The Art and Science of Appreciation, but much of the following brief account can be found in the book by Jamie Goode, *The Science of Wine: From Vine to Glass*.

Our senses of taste and smell work by detecting flavour molecules that interact with receptors in the mouth and in the nasal cavity. In fact, our actual taste buds on the tongue are generally held to be capable of detecting just five different tastes: sweet, salty, bitter, sour and "umami". In contrast, our sense of smell involves hundreds of cells located at the top of our nasal cavity in the "olfactory epithelium", and these can discriminate thousands of different volatile chemical compounds, which we call odours. In fact, olfaction occurs in two ways: *orthonasally*, through the nostrils into the nasal cavity itself, and *retronasally*, via the palate within our mouths. Thus, most of what we somewhat misleadingly call the "taste" of wine in fact stems from this latter route, and is a matter of olfaction, which is why, as any wine taster will tell you, sucking in air and swirling the wine around in your mouth is an important (if rather socially unpleasant) way of "liberating" the volatile flavour compounds of the wine, which then pass through the retronasal passage.

But taste and smell interact in more complex ways than this simple outline suggests, ways that are by no means fully understood. In particular, exactly how they interact in the brain to form our overall experiences of whatever we are eating or drinking is still largely mysterious. The sensory receptor cells in our taste buds and olfactory epithelium convert the chemical information they receive from the compounds in food and drink into electrical signals that then pass into the taste and olfactory cortices in the brain. This is how we recognize what we are smelling and tasting, but it appears that these signals are then combined to create an overall sensation or experience of flavour in a part of the brain called the "orbitofrontal cortex". Importantly, it is here that the pleasantness or unpleasantness – the "hedonic valence" – of what we have ingested is represented (Goode 2005: 176–8).

This neurophysiological account of taste and smell perception is of philosophical significance in so far as it can provide answers to questions such as those we have hitherto touched on, including, in particular: (a) How poor are we at detecting and discriminating tastes and smells? (b) Are there wide and significant variations in our abilities to taste and smell? (c) Can we share the same taste and smell experiences and, in particular, can expert knowledge affect the experience of tasting wine? There seems to be ample scientific evidence to support the sceptical claims of philosophers we encountered in the previous section, for a range of experiments by researchers on the perception of wine seems to yield the conclusion that individuals differ widely in their taste and smell abilities, differences that are both quantitative and qualitative. Just how much variation in sensitivity there is between different individuals is debated, but it is generally accepted that people differ widely in their sensitivity to odours, and each individual shows a range of different thresholds (Goode 2005: 137).

To add yet further variable factors, repeated exposure to the same smell diminishes our sensitivity to it; women may have a heightened sense of smell at ovulation; appetite stimulates smell;

and other factors such as age, gender and atmospheric conditions may all affect smell. In addition, our sensitivity to individual odours in mixtures has been claimed to be extraordinarily limited, even for "normal" perceivers. Goode reports the claim of the researcher David Laing that "Humans can only identify up to a maximum of four odours in a mixture, regardless of whether the odours are a single molecule … or more complex" (Goode 2005: 174).

In addition to variations between individuals' capacity to detect and discriminate smells, Linda Bartoshuk has shown that some people – "supertasters" – are much more sensitive to certain tastes than "normal" tasters (medium tasters), perceiving them more easily and as more intense. Supertasters have a far greater concentration of taste buds than the other groups, and it has been estimated that as much as 25 per cent of the population may be supertasters, and as much as 25 per cent may be "non-tasters", possessing a relatively poor ability to detect certain tastes.

It is not yet known what the implications might be, if any, for wine preferences, and thus far the studies have concentrated on a relatively limited range of stimuli, including quinine, coffee and the chemical phenylthiocarbamide. But it seems clear that different groups of tasters may disagree markedly in their judgements about, for example, the levels of acid, sugar or tannin present in a given wine, and hence whether a wine is balanced. Different groups of individuals may thus have significantly different taste experiences. A supertaster may, for example, perceive a Rheingau Auslese to be as sweet as a Beerenauslese, and where most medium tasters agree that this Barolo is beautifully balanced, structured with firm but velvety tannins, a supertaster may judge its tannins as far too harsh and bitter, resulting in an unbalanced mid-palate. As we shall see later on, the existence of supertasters poses a grave challenge to any defender of the objectivity of taste.

A great deal of recent research on wine perception has examined the various ways in which certain factors such as knowledge, language and expectation play a role in shaping our taste and smell representations. This research can be taken to show further that consumers are prone to making even very simple mistakes about the wine they are consuming, are relatively poor at discriminating and re-identifying wines, and are affected by prior biases and prejudices.

Some experiments by the psychologist Frédéric Brochet demonstrate the influence on taste and smell perception of factors such as vision, memory, expectation and background knowledge. For example, he found that the *very same wine* was subject to very different descriptions by the same group of participants when labelled variously as *vin de table* or *grand cru*. "For the *'grand cru'* wine versus the *'vin de table'*, 'a lot' replaces 'a little'; 'complex' replaces 'simple'; and 'balanced' replaces 'unbalanced'" (Goode 2005: 182). Even more disturbingly, Brochet discovered that colour has an enormous influence on taste perception. Subjects were asked to describe a red and white wine, and a few days later the same white wine, died with a neutral-tasting red food colorant, was re-described in the same terms as the original red wine!

Confirmation of further kinds of bias influencing perception is seen in the "Pepsi challenge" experiment, in which a blind tasting of Pepsi against Coca-Cola under magnetic resonance imaging (MRI) scanning showed a strong initial preference for the former among participants. When told what they were drinking, however, the preferences were reversed and, remarkably, the brain activity also changed, with activity in a region responsible for high-level cognitive processing now lighting up. Apparently, the subjects' knowledge of the brand was shaping their preferences. In the words of Goode:

> The experiments of Brochet and others show that factors such as tasting blind make a crucial difference to the nature of [our perceptual representations of wine], and that representations of the same wine differ markedly among tasters. In addition, the past experiences of tasting will change the nature of our current experiences …
>
> (2005: 182)

All of this research suggests that our taste and smell experiences in general are subject to significant group and individual variations, and that these differences will be exacerbated when directed at complex objects such as wine, the constitution of which consists in a vast mixture of chemical compounds, and the perception of which is subject to a large range of "external" factors, including packaging, background knowledge, memory, experience and expectation, to name but a few. Furthermore, these factors affect not only *what* we taste and smell, what we can identify and discriminate, they also seem to influence the value we attach to tastes and smells. That is, they have a bearing on our preferences and sensory pleasures, and given that these play a significant role in our experiences and judgements of wine – for we do not merely describe, but also evaluate – the philosophical implications for the existence of objectivity and expertise seem damning.

The research seems to challenge the idea that tastes and smells exist objectively in the wine and that we can therefore make anything like objective judgements about them. Despite tasting from the same bottle, there is no interesting sense in which two tasters will be tasting the same tastes and smells, and hence the same wine object. Indeed, it could be claimed that our taste and smell experiences are even more subjective and idiosyncratic than we might have suspected, for there will be as much variation between individual experiences as there are individuals. Moreover, we can, it seems, be mistaken even about our own subjective preferences, given certain background assumptions, expectations and prejudices with which we are burdened and which may even lie beyond our recognition and control.

In sum, the scientific studies appear to support philosophical scepticism about our ability to really know *the* wine object, to attribute real objective smell and taste properties to it. Our judgements of taste and smell are condemned to being ineliminably subjective. If these pessimistic conclusions were true, therefore, there would be little of philosophical interest left in analysing the nature of wine. But one must be wary of drawing simple philosophical conclusions from empirical studies and we should not, I think, be so quick to accept these conclusions.

It is important to note, first, that estimates of the variation in sensitivity between different individuals varies widely and there is not yet sufficient evidence, or sufficient knowledge of taste and smell perception, to pronounce definitively on the exact numbers or the physical causes of these differences with any great conviction. Moreover, it should be emphasized that when it comes to many everyday tastes and smells, there is actually a remarkable amount of agreement in our identifications, and we have no great trouble remembering and re-identifying familiar tastes and odours. Nor does the existence of relatively rare and extreme conditions such as anosmia have any more bearing on the objectivity of taste and smell perception among "normal" tasters than the existence of colour blindness has on the objectivity of colour vision among the vast majority of "normal" colour perceivers. The studies touched on do not show otherwise. They imply, rather, that when it comes to identifying some very specific tastes and smells – such as the bitter-tasting chemical PROP (6-n-propylthioracil) – there are some significant variations between groups.

More importantly, note that the very features held to influence our perceptual taste and smell experiences and preferences are those that in part distinguish experts from non-experts. In 2002, functional MRI brain scans were used to compare the tasting experiences of sommeliers with subjects lacking any specific wine tasting knowledge or abilities. The study showed that there are significant differences between the way in which experts and non-experts analyse and perceive wine. Only in the case of the sommeliers did areas of the brain associated with motivation, memory and cognition light up, suggesting that they were expecting rewards and pleasure from tasting, and were following specific analytic strategies while tasting, including linguistic ones in putting names to flavours. In other words, people familiar with wine tasting seem to experience the tastes and smells of wine differently from those who are not (Goode 2005: 179).

As such, the scientific research by itself does not so much undermine the possibility of expertise as to some extent reinforce it, in so far as it suggests that people with the same background experience, expectations and knowledge may well have the same kinds of experiences when confronted by the same wine, and there may well be people who are better at perceiving tastes and smells than others. In doing so, it poses a direct challenge to Bach's claim that knowledge cannot relevantly affect or enhance our tasting and smelling experiences or the pleasure we derive from them.

Indeed it also reinforces one of the key practices of wine expertise, namely, blind tasting, which is designed specifically to negate the adverse affect that knowledge (and various personal preferences and prejudices) can have on expectation, perception and, particularly, evaluation. For example, knowing in advance that a particular wine comes from a famous producer might incline one to misjudge what is actually, say, an overripe, relatively poor-quality wine in an unduly positive light. Much of the empirical research above has confirmed these kinds of biases, and of course they can function in various ways.

Shamefully, and tragically, my first encounter with Château Cheval Blanc was marred by an imagined distaste for the green pepper aromas associated with Cabernet Franc and present in the (much poorer) Chinon wines with which I was more familiar at the time. As a result, I simply under-appreciated, and indeed failed adequately to taste and understand the rich, complex, powerful and opulent experience this wine could provide.

However, if successful, blind tasting allows accurate judgements of wine to be formed without direct knowledge of what the wine is, to allow it to be judged on its merits, where discerning the character of a wine in this way necessarily presupposes a great deal of implicit knowledge – of a kind to be sketched later – in order to make sense of one's otherwise more or less inchoate perceptual experience. As I noted in the Introduction, the ability of gradually accumulated knowledge and experience to affect what one perceives, and how one evaluates this, is quite remarkable. Learning to differentiate oak from fruit tannins, to assess grape ripeness and natural residual sugar, understanding phenol extraction and malolactic fermentation, all profoundly affect one's tasting and assessment of wine. One learns to appreciate, for instance, what balance is, what wine faults are, and what style in wine is and how to achieve it.

This process is ultimately no more mysterious than, for example, the way in which a radiologist can (and a layman cannot) see a disease in an X-ray, a cricket aficionado can (and a Frenchman cannot) appreciate the delicacy of a leg-glance, or an antiques furniture expert can differentiate and appreciate two chairs that to the non-expert appear completely indistinguishable and unremarkable.

Of course, we have not yet demonstrated that there is such knowledge, that blind tasting is ever accurate, nor have we yet offered a defence of expertise or objectivity. This will come later. But anybody with sufficient experience of blind tasting can be in no doubt about the way in which their background knowledge and experience structures their tasting, influencing their perceptions and judgements in ways – baleful or benign – that provide *prima facie* evidence for the *cognitive penetrability* of wine tasting. One begins to taste *analytically*, looking for particular characteristics of the grape and assessing how the wine has been made, how its elements fit together, what the overall style is, and what sort of quality has been achieved. If one knows in advance that one is tasting a particular varietal, or a wine from a particular region, one will be tasting also to have one's expectations confirmed or confounded.

Here's a typical example from *The World of Fine Wine* reporting a blind tasting comparing the manifestation of the Malbec grape in Cahors and Argentinian wines, and in which overall it was felt that the Argentinian wines were "less of a caricature than we expected. Amid all the oak, dense purple color, and alcohol, there was welcome evidence of greater balance, finesse, and understanding of phenolic ripeness". More specifically, of the Fabre Montemayou Gran Reserva Malbec

2007, one particular taster notes: "Very dense, dark color. High alcohol, roasted, slightly pruney nose. Super-ripe, sweet, Michel Rolland-style. Good fruit picked too late. Super-ripe raisin-and-oak palate. I wish this had 14% alcohol and was not in this over-ripe style."[2] Another taster notes that this is a "big wine that just manages to keep all its powerful elements in proportion, even if at this stage it could do with a couple more years' aging and will continue to improve for 10 years".

The first taster's expert knowledge of the style associated with a particular highly influential oenologist structures his perceptual experience of the wine, allowing the recognition that the fruit is "late-picked" and noting that this, in combination with the particular influence of oak and high alcohol accounts for the sweetness. This knowledge also informs the evaluation of the wine, based on his particular preferences. The fruit is thus perceived to be overripe, the alcohol too high for the style of wine, making it unbalanced, and the use of oak too heavy-handed and overpowering. The second taster's knowledge too allows him to *perceive that* the elements are in proportion and to detect, as it were, the potential in the wine to improve with age. Of course, these tasters appear to disagree in their perceptions and evaluations, so in order to defend the idea that there is genuine knowledge and

---

2. www.finewinemag.com/index.php?action=page&p=sample_features (accessed September 2010). Readers who have seen the film *Mondovino* will be familiar with the controversial Michel Rolland.

accurate judgement in wine tasting we shall have to try eventually to make some sense of what is going on here.

Defending tastes and smells

There can be no doubt that some of this research poses serious challenges to expertise and the objectivity of wine tasting; particularly threatening, I think, are the existence of "supertasters" and, if true, our poor ability to distinguish different odours in a complex mixture. Any attempt to defend the objectivity of wine judgements must somehow explain or incorporate these inconvenient facts into its account, if possible. For the remainder of this chapter, however, we can be content with meeting head-on the philosophical criticisms of tastes and smells.

Recall, first, the differences alleged by some philosophers to hold between the chemical, gustatory senses of taste and smell and the distal senses of sight and hearing, differences used to support the accusation that tastes and smells are not representational, and hence cannot give us access to or information about the world and its objects. In fact, it is quite difficult to know what to make of these claims because they are not supported by clear arguments, but rather are statements about what is supposedly just phenomenologically evident. But it seems equally evident that taste and olfactory capacities do give us information about the world and the objects that emit them. We know through smell when eggs are rotten, and we know through taste that the soup contains salt.

Indeed we could, if we wished, tell a very plausible evolutionary story about just how our senses of taste and smell have developed to alert us to the potential needs, as well as dangers, required to survive.

Sight is held to be an essentially representational sense, through which we have direct access to the world. Yet the notion of representation at work here is far more obscure than such claims imply. In what sense, for example, does the taste of sugar fail to represent sugar or sweetness, the smell of gas fail to represent the gas that is smelled, the disgusting smell of rotting eggs fail to represent their "off-ness", or the classic cigar and cedar smells of claret fail to represent the wine in the glass as a claret? We do not conclude from the fact that someone with hay fever cannot smell the sulphur dioxide that there is nothing there to be smelled, and perhaps we should draw similar conclusions about the cigar and cedar smells in the claret.

Nor does it seem that tastes and smells belong any less to objects than colours and sounds. We smell the bark of the tree as woody in what appears to be just the same kind of way that we see the cushion as blue, hear the note as high, or taste the chocolate as chocolaty. In each case, it is true, we are describing aspects of our experience, but aspects that are clearly anchored in and attached to the physical properties of the world that are causally responsible for those experiences. Of course, these properties need not figure as such in our sensory experiences; we do not see the photons constituting the wavelengths of light responsible for our colour vision any more than we see or smell the chemicals that constitute the smells that we detect. But the objects of our different senses are on a par in this regard.

Colours and sounds, no less than tastes or smells, fall under the umbrella of secondary, response-dependent qualities, but such qualities are still in some sense properties of the object. It is just that they *also* depend on our powers of perception to come fully into being. They are *relational* properties, existing as a relation that holds between us and the world. Nor, further, is it a relevant objection to the objectivity of our taste and olfactory abilities to claim that we can never know whether we have the same taste and smell experiences as others, for the same is true of any experience whatsoever.

Perhaps it is true that the gustatory senses are less well developed, less powerful and less discriminating than our senses of sight and hearing. Given their volatility and chemical composition, tastes and smells – the objects of our gustatory and olfactory perception – may well be more fleeting, difficult to distinguish and remember, more subject to individual variation and more affected by a range of environmental conditions than sights and sounds. For these reasons it may well be more difficult to describe, identify and discriminate them, and they may well lack certain dimensions that sights and sounds possess.

Yet what can we conclude from this? Only that our ability to taste and smell is in some respects inferior to our other sensory abilities, that we find it more difficult to describe and discriminate tastes and smells, and that they are in some respects different from the objects of our other senses. But we can certainly not conclude that there is therefore no power of discrimination at all, that tastes and smells cannot be adequately described, nor that they are entirely subjective and do not in some sense belong to the objects that emit them.

As observation and empirical studies have shown, and as the existence of the wine and perfume industries testify, people can be trained to a high level of olfactory discriminatory ability, which involves improvement in both perception of, and the linguistic ability to describe, tastes and smells. The problematic characteristics of tastes and smells, and our gustatory and olfactory capacities, may well ensure some difficulty in garnering these skills, and ensure that experts may always be few in number. However, it does not show that expertise is impossible, any more than it shows that it is impossible to learn to describe tastes and smells and to capture our experiences in words, as we shall see in the next chapter.

Of course, such expertise would be relatively unimpressive, uninteresting and of limited usefulness if the objects of judgement were themselves relatively simple and uninteresting, incapable of exhibiting order and structure, of possessing expressive qualities or manifesting rewarding aesthetic values, as the philosophical doubters have claimed. But wines and perfumes, I think, provide a clear counter-example to the claim that tastes and smells cannot be structured in ways that exhibit a certain order that can itself be experienced and appreciated as such, and that can bear some of the values attributed to wine.

Perfumiers and *vignerons* talk of their products as possessing various aroma "notes", and even claim that these can be expressed or exhibited temporally due to the temporal volatility of their molecular compounds. So, perfumes can be designed to develop different aromas throughout the day on which they are worn, and wines change and develop over time in both glass and bottle, giving rise to primary, secondary and tertiary aromas and a range of different values in the process. It is in this light that wine tasters talk of first and second "nosings", of the "middle palate", of "attack" and "finish".

Does this talk correspond accurately to objective development, change and succession in the world? The change and development of aromas clearly has some basis in the temporal nature of chemical volatility, so why not take the claims of manufacturers at face value and agree that tastes and smells in complex objects such as wine can be structured and arranged in the ways they obviously seem to be in order to manifest the sorts of qualities of which wine is capable, and for which it is valued? Some of the qualities intrinsic to wine are, therefore, qualities of order and temporal transition. A good wine, for example, will open up after time in the glass to reveal new layers of properties; the extremely rich and powerful cassis, cedar and smoky first nose of a Château Haut-Brion 1986 will give way to subtler aromas of chocolate, spices, coffee, tobacco and roses, all of which will hint at the burly but elegantly rounded palate of powerful but smooth tannins, concentrated black fruit, clear steely minerality and incredibly long finish. A temporal depth of structure, on the nose and palate, has been revealed, and the wine is assessed according to the harmony and balance achieved among the rich and complex interplay of its many tastes and smells, as well as the length and intensity of its finish.

As we shall discuss in further detail later, it is important to note that these are not simply incidental features of fine wines, but are in large part the result of skill, intention and an understanding of values intrinsic to the nature of wine. Indeed, in these ways, wines are clearly capable of generating at least expectation and harmony. A wine can, for instance, fail to live up to the complexity detected on the first nose when eventually circulated around the palate (or for that matter garnered from prior knowledge of its production); conversely, it can promise such complexity and after some time deliver or exceed it. These are simply straightforward examples of everyday occurrences when wine tasting, and undermine the idea that tastes and smells are necessarily free-floating, unrelated and too easily and confusingly mixed.

So, what is the wine object? Is it independent of our taste and smell experiences or somehow necessarily dependent on and constituted by them? The answer, as we shall see, is "both", but I think that even at this early stage in our investigation it is not implausible to say that our smells and tastes of wine *represent the wine object* in a way directly akin to the way visual experiences are held to represent objects in the world.

Of course, if one were utterly unfamiliar with wine, one might smell and taste it without the experience being *of* wine, and hence conceptualized as such. But all this demonstrates is the possibility of failing to appreciate the wine *as* wine, and those tastes and smells *as* wine tastes and smells. When smelling and tasting with the right kind of knowledge and experience, however, we are truly representing the wine, and our taste and smell experiences will constitute knowledge of it. There is, I want to say, tasting and smelling *with understanding*. If so, taste and smell perception can be *veridical* in just the way that philosophers have held belongs properly only to vision. Such experiences, that is, can possess a notion of "correctness", allowing us to distinguish objects in the world from our experiences of them and thereby granting to our judgements of wine some measure of objectivity. It is now time to see how this is so.

2

The Language of Wine
Chemicals, Metaphors and Imagination

Ways with words

"Nuts, spice, liquorice, herbs, very complex, lots of body and depth to the fruit, with well-defined mineral accents." "Silky, stylish, sexy – but also elegant, tight, and finely tuned."

"Beautifully poised with lively acidity and tightly coiled tannins."

"Attractive and forward, fresh acidity but lovely breadth of fruit on mid-palate."

"A racy little number, fresh and perky with vigorous fruit."

"Extrovert, handsome, and charming, destined to be head of school."

"This vintage is for cellaring not drinking, but this example already has sufficient concentration to convince that it will make a memorable bottle in three or four years".

"It will never win a race but it's a wonderful little jogger."
"Charming, vibrant wine that demonstrates the family's
painstaking winemaking style well."[1]

The vast array of ways in which wine can be described defies
straightforward analysis, but chances are, given that you are reading
this book, you will already be familiar with the enormous pan-
orama of wine characterizations, and the examples above are
designed merely to give some flavour of this. They range from
the simple, literal and descriptive to the elaborate, metaphorical
and evaluative, through to the imaginative, outlandish and absurd.
They encompass judgements referring not just to what we might
call "intrinsic" features of the wine, but also "extrinsic" features
such as winemakers' intentions and values, styles of wine, and pre-
dictions about future characteristics that can be tasted now, as it
were, as latent potential in the wine.

In Chapter 1 we discussed whether our taste and smell experiences of wine could provide us with genuine knowledge of the
wine object itself, or whether when apparently judging and attributing properties to it we are really doing no more than reporting
our subjective experiences. The sceptical challenge consisted in
holding that tastes and smells were secondary qualities that could
not represent a world beyond themselves, and various characteristics were given as evidence of this, such as their chemical, ephem-

---

1. I have taken these wine descriptions more or less at random from a number
   of places, including Sibley (2001), and www.jancisrobinson.com.

eral and unstable nature, our relatively poor ability to perceive, discriminate and recall them, and the purportedly impoverished scope of our vocabulary to describe them.

In order to address these issues more directly it is crucial to gain a clearer understanding of the connection between wine and words, of how wine language is employed, whether smells, tastes and wines can be accurately described, and whether the judgements listed above can be appropriate or true. The mere thimbleful of examples given above might seem to go some way to belying claims about the impoverished vocabulary at our disposal to describe tastes and smells, as well as their supposed immunity to structure and order. But everyday scepticism about the practice of wine appreciation and expertise stems directly from the strong feeling that such an apparently straightforward sensory object simply cannot bear the exotic and flowery language bestowed upon it. This worry clearly supports the further idea that when offering such descriptions we are really just describing our own subjective impressions and experiences: descriptions that, with few or no constraints on imaginative embellishment, may all too easily sever whatever bonds were tethering them to mundane worldly objects and take flight into the realms of fantasy.

The key questions for us to consider, therefore, are how wine vocabulary emerges, how it is used and, most importantly, whether the words used to characterize wine can be anchored more or less firmly in objective properties of the wine, or perhaps in objective properties of our shared experiences of it. What, if anything, separates the appropriate from the absurd?

It is important first to be alert to two important distinctions among the many different ways in which we attribute smells and tastes to wine. The first distinction is that between *descriptive* and *evaluative* judgements about wine, and the second between *literal* and *metaphorical* descriptions of wine tastes and smells.

The first distinction should seem obvious enough. An example of a straightforward description of wine would be "this Beaujolais is acidic on the palate and smells of blueberries and bubblegum", while an evaluation would be "the Beaujolais is a good one". A further distinction that will be important for our later discussion of objectivity is that between *evaluation* and expressions of *preference*. The former attributes qualities/values to the wine, and the latter expresses a liking or disliking for such qualities. It *looks* perfectly legitimate to claim on the one hand that, for instance, the Beaujolais is a good wine, well made, balanced and demonstrating an impressive range of characteristics essentially belonging to its type, but on the other hand say that I personally do not like it, it is not to my taste. I may prefer wines, no matter how well made, to be fuller bodied and not to smell faintly of bubblegum. Of course, appearances can be deceptive and whether there is a genuine distinction here is something we need to demonstrate, but note for the moment merely that *preferences* – but not necessarily evaluations – are irreducibly *subjective* in that they are essentially *about* our subjective experiences.

I take it, too, that the notion of literal description is unproblematic. Such descriptions will apply literally to the wine; that is, the wine will really possess the actual qualities literally attributed to it, which may for example include attributions of bitterness and acidity to the taste, or the smell of spiciness or fruitiness to what is smelled. Metaphorical descriptions, on the other hand, will be ways of characterizing tastes and smells that cannot be literally true of these objects. Examples will include attributions of human characteristics such as "masculine" or "shy" to wines. And finally, evaluations (not just descriptions) of wine may also be divided between the literal and metaphorical. "Well balanced" might turn out to be a literal evaluation of properties actually possessed by "good" wines, while "sexy" or "charming" appear to be metaphorical evaluations.

Yet as even these simple examples intimate, the lines separating the literal from the metaphorical, and even the descriptive from the evaluative, are by no means always clear-cut. Some metaphors can become "dead" or conventionalized to the point where they act as straightforward literal descriptions, as we shall see below, while some *prima facie* evaluative terms, such as "elegant", "over-ripe", "flabby", "charming", may consist of certain descriptive components. "Flabby", for example, is primarily used to describe wines that are lacking in the acidity necessary to give them sufficient body. As such, it is both a description of certain properties – or lack of properties – in a wine, as well as an evaluation of wine quality. Or take, for example, the judgement "the honeyed sweetness of the Château Filhot is elegantly balanced with a subtle yet satisfying backbone of crisp acidity". Is this descriptive or evaluative, or both? Similar grey areas beset the distinction between the literal and the metaphorical. On which side does the judgement "the Pinot Grigio is clean and crisp, with a bright and breezy lemony nose" fall?

Nobody has done more to bring the language of wine to the world's attention than Adrienne Lehrer, who, in the book *Wine and Conversation* (2009), provides comprehensive analyses of wine vocabulary, a semantic account of "winespeak" and the various functions of wine talk, and an outline of a range of blind tasting experiments performed on various groups, designed specifically to examine these topics. A quick overview of these experiments is useful, I feel, in showing both the significant differences in judgement between experts and non-experts, and yet also the vagaries inherent in these empirical tests.

In Lehrer's first set of experiments, one group consisted of wine scientists from the University of California at Davis, while the other groups were not wine experts. Lehrer showed that the Davis Group used significantly different descriptor terms and consistently outperformed the other groups on a range of tasks, including consensus on the meanings of terms applied to wine, and on the descriptions appropriate to a given wine. They did not, however, perform better at matching a wine to another person's descriptions of that wine, except when allowed to refer to colour and appearance and when tasting wines with which they were familiar, namely, Californian varietals (Lehrer 2009: 167).

In a series of later experiments, by herself and others, performed primarily to test differences between experts and non-experts, Lehrer reports that experts were again found to do significantly better at matching their own descriptions than non-experts. They also appeared to demonstrate a greater ability to discriminate flavour and aroma, leading them to distinguish more successfully between wines. However, in many of these tests the experimenters also drew the conclusion that although experts perform statistically better than non-experts, they do not necessarily perform impressively better, and there was noticeable disagreement in communication concerning the words used to describe wine even among experts.

What should we conclude from this? Perhaps the most that we can say is that, as Lehrer says, "translating taste and aroma experiences into language is very difficult" and that "to become an expert requires not only an outstanding ability to taste and smell, but an extraordinary memory for taste and smell as well" (186). Does "noticeable disagreement" undermine objectivity? What explains the level and types of agreement and disagreement among experts? How much, and what type, of disagreement would suffice to undermine expertise and objectivity? Do the experiments show that experts perceive more, or merely that they are better at describing what they, and everybody else, perceive? Some of these questions echo issues raised in Chapter 1, and an exploration of some others must wait until Chapters 3 and 4, but they suggest that when it comes to establishing philosophical conclusions, the empirical evidence here is very far from clear or sufficient. We can, however, turn to empirical evidence to begin to understand what grounds some of our judgements about the properties of wine.

Words and chemicals

Why do we say that this Grands Échezaux smells of crystallized violets, that the Sancerre smells of cat's pee, the Alsatian Gewürztraminer has a strong lychee and slightly herbaceous aroma, and the Fleurie a first nose of bubblegum? The obvious response is "because they do!" More precisely, we smell these things because there are volatile chemical compounds present in the wine that are the same as, or relevantly similar to, those that are present in the substances to which we refer when describing wines in these ways.

As we noted in Chapter 1, nothing like a comprehensive list of the enormous range of chemicals present in complex objects such as wine has yet been compiled, partly owing to the sheer number, and partly to the complexity and volatility of the olfactory compounds involved. But the state of knowledge of such compounds is growing rapidly and there seems to be nothing, in principle, to stop an eventual identification of all of them.

It is obvious that many of the literal descriptive judgements we make about wine will be objective in applying straightforwardly to chemical characteristics of the wine. Moreover, if there were no such correlation, winemakers would have little control over the character of their product, and the decisions so crucial to crafting something that will be successful and appreciated in the ways intended would be rendered futile. Many of these correlates have now been classified, some arising from particular fermentation techniques and the particular varieties of yeast active in this, some based in winemaking techniques and materials, such as those involved in the various stages of *elevage*, and many others lying in the properties of the grape varieties themselves.

For example, Muscat wines receive their distinctive floral character from the presence of linalool and geraniol in Muscat grapes, while the herbaceous, grassy, sometimes peppery aromas found in Cabernet Sauvignon and Sauvignon Blanc wines stem from specific methoxypyrazine compounds that are also found in these substances. The typical oaky or woody aromas and tastes present in white Burgundies will probably be a direct result of the chardonnay grapes having been fermented and aged in oak barrels that have directly imparted their oak lactones. Some oak – American oak in particular – contains the compound ethyl vanillate, which is also present in vanilla and which gives some oaked wines, such as Rioja, their distinctly vanilla odour. The leathery and gamey aromas often found in Rhone Syrahs are frequently the products of the yeast *Brettanomyces*. Similarly, we can attribute the tastes in wine – the astringency of tannin, the sweetness of sugar, acidity – to the various chemical properties responsible for these, such as polyphenols, anthocyanics, glucose and so on.

From this basis it is a more or less straightforward matter to match individual tastes and smells to the kinds of wine that typically possess them. German Rieslings, for instance, typically have a kerosene nose that is unmistakable, and clarets typically have equally unmistakable pencil shavings and cedar aromas. Some of these characteristics will be due to the grape variety, some to the winemaking techniques.

We may, at times, refer directly to the chemical make-up of the wine itself, as when we say for example that "this Syrah is low in malic acid, high in phenols and extract". But of course, unless we are providing a scientific analysis, we will generally give descriptions that in a more or less direct way refer to chemicals that we name via association with the familiar substances in which they occur. For we are not interested merely in naming, but in meaningfully describing. That is, there would be little point in using chemical names to *describe* the smells and tastes of wine, for such names do not help us capture and communicate our perceptual experiences. Obviously, however, we would not expect to find cat's pee or wet cardboard actually in the wine we describe as emitting such aromas, but we would expect to find chemical compounds common to both the wine and the substance in virtue of which it smells to us the way that it does.

Describing odours in terms of the substances that they resemble, and of which they remind us, thus has a chemical basis that *grounds* the *literal use and meaning* of such descriptions. These range from the broad and generic – for example floral, vegetative, pungent – to the specific – for example oaky, buttery, peppery, honeyed, burnt toast, wet cardboard. It is thus possible to provide some standardization and categorization for such descriptions, and to apply them to specific wine types. This is exactly what has been done, for instance, in the well-known "aroma wheel" developed by Ann C. Noble at the University of California, Davis.[2]

---

2. See www.winearomawheel.com. Variations on this wheel can also be found in many introduction to wine tasting books, and there's a particularly nice example in Robinson (2003), which matches specific tastes and smells to the wines and grape varieties that typically manifest them.

So, the objectivity of the literal descriptions of tastes and smells in wine is in large part secured by a firm empirical basis. And it is important to note that this basis is primarily a *causal* one. That is, these properties do not seem to require any knowledge or interpretation to be detected; we simply perceive them unless we are suffering from a condition that interferes with this causal route, much as I would not perceive colours accurately if I were wearing rose-tinted spectacles or became partially colour-blind.

If you do not smell the honeyed, floral character of the Beaumes-de-Venise, or taste its sweetness on the palate, you are failing to detect what is there to be detected, and the fault lies – for whatever reason, perhaps you have a cold – with you. And we could, in principle, *demonstrate this empirically*.

Of course, none of this should come as a great surprise. What is surprising, rather, is that people should doubt the legitimacy of even these types of literal descriptions. Given the vast number and interactions of the volatile compounds in such a complex product as wine, why should we not expect it to yield all the sensations the experts claim to detect? Given this volatility, interaction and complexity, and granted those fragile features of tastes and smells outlined in Chapter 1, we should also not be surprised that describing our taste and smell experiences of wine is very difficult, but that if our vocabulary in this area is limited, there is no reason to think that this is anything but a contingent matter. We do not, as it happens, generally make the admittedly large effort required to learn to discriminate and describe tastes and smells in the way we perhaps do with sights and sounds. If this effort is made, however, as it is by experts, it is clear that there is nothing about our perceptual ability itself to discriminate tastes and smells that suggests we could not in principle put a great many names to a great many substances if we so chose. It should be unsurprising that this requires, like anything, a certain degree of knowledge, experience, training and, crucially, a developed standardized vocabulary (Sibley 2001).

Nor, given these features, should it be unexpected that we encounter more disagreements (if we do) about the smells and tastes in wine than in judgements about sights and sounds. Naturally, they may require some practice and experience to be distinguished within the complex mixture that is the wine, but the crucial point is that, for at least a broad range of simple perceptual taste and smell properties, such expertise does not seem to secure the mere ability to perceive them in the first place.

As you might expect, matters are not quite as straightforward as I've just presented them. For, when tasting wine, we move quickly and obscurely from the literal to the metaphorical and from the straightforward causal perception of certain taste and smell properties to the "perception" of features that appear to be partly evaluative, and to involve knowledge and interpretation; features, that is, that are not *just perceived*, but the perception of which requires something in addition to a well-functioning nose and palate. Here, it seems, disagreements become more marked and the language of experts increasingly difficult to assess for meaning and accuracy, if it is to be so assessed at all. Perhaps there is less perception at work than imagination and whimsy.

Experts and metaphors

When it comes to describing the complex mixtures of tastes and smells, structured in the various and deliberate ways that we find in wine, the limited scope of devices such as the aroma wheel in capturing wine's qualities and values is evident. In particular, when it comes to capturing in words the structure and "mouthfeel" of wines, and the overall combination of aromas, tastes, textures, body and finish, that *is* the wine experience, the use of figurative and metaphorical language is indispensable.

Perhaps the most striking ways in which wines are typically characterized is in their personification; that is, wines are attributed human characteristics and personality. Physically, wines can be big, bold, corpulent, fleshy, skeletal, muscular, masculine, feminine, thin, emaciated. They can be gentle, inviting, cheerful, pretentious, amusing, enticing, proud, vicious, capricious, sly, shy, restrained, voluptuous. Wines can be straightforward, clean, genuine, authentic, honest, pure, commercial. They can possess or lack virtues and vices, and they can be precocious, chic, raunchy, demure, smart, elegant, charming, sophisticated, refined, brilliant, distinguished, gracious, enticing, sumptuous, seductive, opulent – and their opposites. Expressions are even used, as Émile Peynaud (1987: ch. 9) says, to define a wine's place in an elite vinous "society" – noble, rich, uncouth, vulgar, plebeian, poor, everyday, pedestrian, unpretentious. They can be energetic, vigorous, spirited, powerful, combative, aggressive, feeble, puny, lacking backbone. Are such descriptions necessarily subjective, arbitrary, silly, pretentious, inappropriate, false? How could wines possibly possess human-like qualities? Could it ever be appropriate to call a wine extroverted, feminine, capricious, rustic or joyful?

These are tricky questions, to which a short answer must for the time being suffice: the appropriateness or correctness of metaphorical descriptions is ultimately justified by the reasons that can be given to support them, and one obvious set of reasons that can do at least part of the required job here are those perceptible properties literally possessed by wines. Some metaphors, that is, can be justified where they can be *reduced to* – that is, entirely explicated in terms of – such properties (Sibley 2001: 248; Smith 2007b: 58–9; Bender 2008: 129–30; Lehrer 2009: ch. 6).

This can perhaps most easily be seen in the case of simple properties that we can taste directly and that can be empirically measured, such as the acidity of a wine, which produces a biting, sharp feeling along the sides of the tongue. There does not seem to be any other way of describing this effect – the taste and feel of acidity – except by using words such as "biting" or "sharp" or "crisp", for which reason these have arguably ceased to be metaphorical at all. But they quickly bring other metaphors in their train. So the acidity in a wine can readily be described as sharp or dull, lively or flat, firm or flabby, and the character of a wine will depend in part on these features and their interactions with other features.

The fluid, natural way in which metaphors expand and give rise to further metaphors, borrowing terms from related areas by a process of inexorable association, is a familiar enough phenomenon, as we can see in examining the "vocabulary of structure" and the "vocabulary of taste", in which impressions of volume, form and consistency on the palate are conveyed in terms of three-dimensional body and shape.

Tasters talk of a wine's profile, its contours and architecture, design and structure and balance. The lastingness of its shape is described as long or short, its overall size as big or small, its volume as slight, ample, imposing. A wine is formless if its image on the palate is unclear, or it might be rounded, angular, flat. A wine lacking body can be thin, slender, graceful, hollow, skimpy, light, threadbare. Full-bodied wines can be complete, stout, heavy, thick. On the tongue, wines that are rich and sweet can be satiny, silky, velvety, woolly, slick, flowing. Others can be aggressive, harsh, rough, cutting, coarse. A wine's consistency is partly a result of its degree of solidity, a texture perceived by the mouth's tactile sense. It distinguishes wines that are hard, firm, unyielding and severe from those that are gentle, supple, melting, soft, suave, mellowed. Wines with a solid consistency are those answering the descriptions pulpy, rich, gummy, sticky, unctuous, pasty, cloying, oily, viscous (Peynaud 1987: ch. 9).

As should be clear from even a cursory glance at some of these terms, the boundary between the literal and metaphorical is relatively fluid and continuous. For example, descriptions of mouth-feel and texture, such as "satiny" or "velvety", appear to operate like the aroma terms "buttery" or "peppery" insofar as they highlight properties that are perceptually similar to the objects to which such terms are primarily applied: velvet and satin cloth. Arguably, such terms may not be best understood as metaphorical, but literal.

Many of these descriptions and terms are applied with direct reference to certain measurable empirical qualities that are detected on the palate, in combination with certain olfactory sensations. For example, a wine that is full-bodied has consistency, and this is linked to its content of polyphenols, alcohol and dry extract. The body of a wine may be reinforced by alcoholic strength, but the impression of body is due to certain dissolved substances, to the extract and sapid complex of acids and tannins. Vinosity is what gives wine its strength and vigour. A strong wine is high in alcohol, and appropriately labelled robust, hefty, beefy, whereas its opposite will be weak, puny, lightweight.

These correlations between chemical properties and metaphors can even be extended to capture more elusive psychological human character attributes. An interesting example is given by Lehrer, concerning the word "pretentious":

> A pretentious person is one who pretends to have a background, pedigree, education, or other qualities that he does not have. It should be possible to interpret a *pretentious* wine as one that looked, tasted, smelled, and felt like an aged Château Lafite but was really a jug wine from San Joaquin Valley selling for $1.89 a gallon … However, the connotation of *pretentious* is negative, so that a pretentious wine could not be really as good as a fine one. An expert

would be able to tell that the noble qualities were lacking. Therefore, a pretentious wine would probably have to be fairly expensive and be labelled to imitate a wine that was better.   (2009: 31)

So, the relevant properties detected by taste and smell help justify the correct application of the relevant metaphors, thereby making their meanings and usage subject to truth and falsity – or "truth-apt" as philosophers say – and hence grounding the objectivity of judgements involving them. As we can see from this last example, however, even if many metaphors can be grounded in, and hence partially justified by reference to, perceptible properties or sets of properties in the wine that could be readily detected by "ordinary" tasters, this is in many cases insufficient to establish their appropriateness or truth – to give them their "truth-conditions". Why?

First, because the correct use of such metaphors further requires some level of agreement about their application, agreement which in some cases won't be found by asking "ordinary" tasters. Second, because many such metaphors cannot be directly paraphrased in terms of – wholly reduced to – basic perceptible properties. They possess a meaning over and above their reference to such properties. Specifically, many are partly or wholly *evaluative* and refer to certain subjective experiences of value, the precise connection of which to objective properties of the wine is an extremely thorny and tangled affair that we can begin only to prune in the remainder of this chapter, and which will concern

61

us in greater depth in Chapters 3 and 4. But here are some brief observations to ponder.

Whatever one's philosophical or linguistic theory of meaning, it is clear that experts play a fundamental role in determining the meaning and application of terms to wines. Whether terms are applied accurately or not will depend in part on the agreement of experts, and this agreement is needed to secure the reference of terms to properties in the first place. Once there is sufficient agreement about the use of certain terms, and the perceptual properties to which they are applied, these can become *conventional* within the framework of talking about wine, with agreed standards for correct use. It is in this light, too, that experts will be able to explain why the wine has the characteristics that is does and what to expect of certain wines, and to differentiate wine styles. Thus, where such conventions and consensus are in play, the objectivity of judgements is to some extent secure (*ibid.*: 77).

If someone, for instance, were to judge a Rheingau Riesling that was in fact high in acidity as flabby and flat, or a young and powerfully concentrated and tannic Hermitage as feminine or delicate, they would be straightforwardly wrong, either in virtue of misperceiving the properties of the wine or misusing the vocabulary. If one were unsure what exactly somebody meant by calling a wine muscular, we could simply ask them for their justifying reasons and expect to receive an answer citing, for instance, the astringency of the tannins and their relationship to the viscosity of the wine, its alcoholic kick and concentrated fruit.

We should thus expect a high level of agreement and standardization of use with respect to the application of certain metaphors that have direct correlations with the empirical, perceptible properties of wine. This correlation is, after all, what allows winemakers to produce wines with certain specific characteristics, and for consumers to be informed of what they can expect when wines are described in certain ways.

One important dimension of complexity here is that many of the adjectives applied to wine are gradable, or scalar, terms: that is, they admit of degrees. So, for example, to call a wine heavy or sweet, smooth or tannic, young or old, raises questions such as the following: heavy in relation to what? How much sugar does a wine have to possess in order to be sweet? Sometimes these judgements will be made simply with reference to certain physiological preferences and thresholds: "this wine is just too sweet to drink, it's more like grape juice than wine". But frequently, and especially where more complex judgements of fine wine are being made, such terms must be analysed as involving implicit comparisons made against an appropriate reference class with an assumed norm.

These reference classes may be very broad – for example "red wine" – or very narrow – for example "Sonoma Valley Pinot Noir". When judgements with scalar terms are made – for example "the Auslese is lacking a little depth and sweetness" – they must be understood as involving an implicit "for wines of type x"; that is, a norm (or norms) that govern the type of wine at issue and against which our experiences of it are, as it were, measured. What counts as sweet for a Riesling Auslese may not count as sweet for a

Tokay, or for a Riesling Trockenbeerenauselse (*ibid.*: 67–8). Judgements explicitly about, or implicitly drawing on, such reference classes form the backbone of expertise, and even a cursory glance at any wine magazine will reveal a littering of statements such as "a perfect expression of the Margaux vineyard", or "massive structure for a Haut-Brion".

How are these norms established? In part, by the experts, for they are the people familiar with the nature and variety of wine types, and who have honed their powers of discrimination through training and experience; but also partly by the particular conventions in force in a given wine-drinking culture. In other words, the norms governing the correctness of judgements are (i) established by the existence of certain conventions that in turn govern the use of wine language, and (ii) relative to the experts whose agreement supports, and is in turn supported by, these very conventions.

This might look unhelpfully circular – Who determines what level of agreement counts as sufficient? What happens when there is disagreement? – but for the moment we can note that each component of this picture is ultimately grounded in perceptible properties of the wine that are, in principle, available to be checked against the judgements of experts. These properties constrain the metaphorical judgements that can be made about them. This is an important point, because for some gradable terms that are partly evaluative there will be certain physiological thresholds correlated with certain objective conditions that help govern their correct application.

To this extent the establishment of norms and standards governing the use of metaphorical judgements in the wine world does not appear to be saliently different *in kind* from the way in which expertise grounds linguistic usage in other evaluative areas of discourse where implicit norms are also operative, such as those in sport, art or haute cuisine. But the appearance is partially deceptive, because research seems to indicate that even purported wine experts may not always be judging relative to the same norms, that personal preferences have strong sway over how norms are interpreted and applied, and hence that they may therefore often be talking at cross-purposes. In this light we should thus expect to see widespread disagreement across the class of metaphorical judgements. Brochet, for instance, takes his own experiments on the role of words in the psychology of tasting among wine experts to demonstrate the following (Goode 2005: 181):

(i) The authors' descriptive representations are based on the types of wines and not on the different parts of the tasting.

(ii) Representations are "prototypical": that is, specific vocabularies are used to describe types of wines, and each vocabulary represents a type of wine.

(iii) The range of words used is different for each author.

(iv) Tasters possess a specific vocabulary for preferred and non-preferred wines.

(v) Cultural information is present in the sensorial descriptions.

What are we to make of these claims? At this stage I think it is too difficult to give a unified account of the many ways in which metaphors and evaluations are, or are not, grounded in perceptible properties and relative to specific conventions and norms to which all wine experts, in principle, have access and which they deploy in their judgements. The features of wine metaphors we have hitherto examined seem to indicate a kind of continuum of agreement, ranging from the very specific, literal and descriptive to the more evaluative and metaphorical. Determining how rigidly grounded in conventions and agreement are the judgements towards the latter end of the spectrum would require detailed considerations on a case-by-case basis.

Of the Château Lafite Rothschild 2009, for instance, many tasters would agree with Steven Spurrier's note: "Black purple red, elegant concentration of pure Lafite Cabernets, wild violets, succulent yet restrained fruit, both fleshy and firm, superb middle palate, not massively structured but like a Gothic cathedral: austere on the outside and soaring to great heights in the inside".[3] How widespread and *normal* is the Gothic cathedral metaphor? This is obviously an empirical, rather than philosophical, question, but in any case it is clear enough that we can, given the description of the properties of the wine, make perfect sense of it and this will ultimately be the key to understanding the objectivity and correctness of metaphorical judgements.

---

3. www.decanter.com/wine/finder/Chateau-Lafite-Rothschild--1er-Cru-Classe--Pauillac/72305 (accessed September 2010).

For this reason, I think that establishing how wine metaphors in general *can be* true or false, relative to perceptible properties, expertise, norms and conventions is sufficient to side step some of the sceptical claims we have raised.

In order to make these ideas a little more concrete, let's look at the use of the term "balanced", which is central to assessing the structure and value of wine. Now to be at a minimum standard drinkable, wine must be structured of a number of elements such that it is not too bitter, astringent, sweet or alcoholic. In so far as the elements constituting it can be to a large extent empirically determined, the term "balanced" can be applied literally and descriptively. So, in the case of red wines, the sweetness of certain substances (alcohol, glycerol, fermentable sugars) should balance the sum of acid tastes and those of tannic substances. Adequately acidic and tannic wines will be fresh and well structured, whereas wines without sufficient acidity or tannin will be "flabby" and "thin". There seem to be, in these respects, certain empirical thresholds governing balance in wine, thresholds relative to our taste and smell perception and to the properties in the wine to which they correspond.

On the other hand, however, although it may take relatively minimal knowledge and experience to attribute balance to wine, "balanced" is clearly also an *evaluative* term that depends partly on certain preferences. Some philosophers here make a distinction between "thick" and "thin" terms or concepts. The former are terms that are partly evaluative and partly descriptive. More precisely, their evaluative part has more or less clear descriptive criteria for its application. "Balanced" is a paradigmatic "thick" term, in that it can only be correctly applied where certain definite conditions are in place, as given above, but the full meaning of it is not exhausted by pointing just to the physical properties of the wine. We need also to make reference to the evaluative experiences of drinkers. Moreover, what counts as being balanced will itself be relative to different wine types and styles; what counts as balanced for white wines will be different from balance in red wine.

Now some of these subjective values and preferences may be widely shared, and perhaps they are even cross-cultural. For example it seems to be universally agreed that certain properties of wine, such as being oxidized or possessing mercaptans, constitute wine faults. Some preferences, on the other hand, may be culturally (or, more narrowly, "community") relative. For example, many view the presence of *Brettanomyces* as an indication of a wine fault, but some of the best vintages of Beaucastel have apparently been infected with higher than threshold levels of "brett", and many also hold that this has been responsible for certain positively valued characteristics of the wine, in particular its earthy, animal-like scent (Goode 2005: ch. 18).

Some values and preferences, however, may be shaped by and relative to certain norms and conventions that are the preserve of only small groups of experts. This will often be the case where the relevant comparison classes are very narrow. Judging the balance of a Cahors, for instance, might require a great deal of knowledge and experience drinking this particular type of wine. Concomitantly, the metaphors applied to Cahors will be subject to norms known only to relatively few.

Yet other values and preferences may be relative to individuals and hence the metaphors used in judgements to express them will be, to that extent, subjective and idiosyncratic. In these cases, it seems that we could not expect to secure objectivity or agreement, and if such cases were significantly many, and present even among experts, the sceptical claims of Chapter 1 would return to haunt us. Perhaps, after all, when indulging in metaphorical flights of fancy, experts are simply describing their own subjective experiences, making things up as they go, rather than providing insight into the wine itself. The existence of these latter types of case would be worrying if they constituted the norm, but it's far from obvious to me that they do, and I think the burden of proof here falls on the sceptic to show otherwise.

Talking about experiences

The idea to be explored in this final section is that some of our wine talk is not as directly about the wine itself as implied by our discussion hitherto, but rather at least in part about our experiences of it. Some writers have observed that wine discourse shares some important features with aesthetic discourse, an observation that is obvious with a little reflection, for many of the values we attribute to wine appear to be aesthetic in nature: charming, beautiful, elegant, harmonious, expressive and so on.

Drawing on Arnold Isenberg's well-known account of the function of art criticism, which is to bring the perceiver to hear or see – to *experience* – the artwork in a certain way, Lehrer (2009: 214) argues that the aim of some of our wine discourse is similar insofar as it functions not so much to make true and objective statements about the wine, but rather to "critically communicate" our experiences to others. This kind of experience, she holds, is particularly relevant to understanding the meaning of evaluative terms applied to wine.

It is worth noting that a number of philosophers writing on wine have also stressed the importance of the experience of wine in our appreciation and judgements of it. Ophelia Deroy (2007: 117–18), for example, has argued that such appreciation involves a global, rather than piecemeal, analytic experience of the object and as such cannot be reduced to a purely scientific list of its chemical composition. John Dilworth (2008: 87), like Lehrer, draws on aesthetic experience and the assessment of artworks for a model, claiming that in talk of art and wine there is an important distinction to be made between what he calls the "imaginative, representational meaning", which is essentially to do with the experience of wine, and the "literal meaning" attached simply to the description of sensory qualities.[4]

---

4. Such accounts also appear to have some support from the scientific research mentioned already, where the "representation" of wine is processed as a "global form, integrating, on equal terms, chemosensorial, visual, imaginary, and verbal imagination" (Goode 2005: 182).

The connection between wine and art is one we shall return to, but the general idea present in these reflections is this: that the meaning of evaluative terms, including metaphors, is often completed by reference to experiences; that such experiences are not reducible to simple chemosensory perception of the physical properties of the wine; and that it is these experiences that one hopes to get others to share through using the relevant metaphorical terms. This seems to me to be eminently plausible, and many of the terms used to describe wine clearly function to convey *both* characteristics of the wine *and* the experiences to which such characteristics give rise: "sensually expressive", "ethereal", "clean", "expansive", "voluptuous" and so on.

The role of experience is also no doubt partly responsible for the suggestibility to which one is often subject when trying to figure out precisely what one is smelling and tasting, or how best to characterize it. It also explains why the use of certain words might lead a taster to notice the feature that he or she might have missed without hearing the description. That is to say, it provides an account of how our experiences are, as we saw briefly in Chapter 1, *cognitively penetrable*. What we smell and taste is influenced by what we know, believe and think. In this case, what we taste and smell and judge is affected, moulded and shaped in part by the words we, and others, use to describe these very experiences. No doubt, too, there is something intrinsically valuable in the nature of the sharing itself that provides an important reason for conversing in the ways that we do. It is more valuable to drink and discourse with others than alone.

Yet even here, where truth is supposedly not the central issue, there are constraints in operation that govern, however loosely, the experiences that can be shared. Naturally, some wines simply won't support certain types of ascriptions. Calling a very complex and sophisticated wine such as a Chave Hermitage Blanc a "wonderful little jogger" would be an indication that we had entered the world of parody, and it would be stretching language and physiology beyond what they can bear to attempt to *describe* or *experience*, for example, a heavily alcoholic, monstrously tannic and unbalanced Australian Shiraz as "delicate and feminine".

Just how much imaginative flexibility and creativity can our shared experiences bear? Just enough, I think, to give some indication of why appreciating wine is so valuable, but also to intimate that the primary function of wine discourse is not, as Lehrer suggests, to share experiences devoid of the ideal of truth. Truth is, I think in some form, always relevant. Jancis Robinson, for instance, has recently described the 2009 Cheval Blanc as "Almost like a child told to concentrate and do its piano practice":[5] an outlandish description, you might think, but actually quite well justified by her full description of the wine:

Very rich and comfortable on the nose. Very juicy. Dry finish. Very serious wine. Lots of layers and a dry finish.

---

5. Quoted at www.bbr.com/product-76453B-ch-cheval-blanc-st-emilion?list_tab_F=RI (accessed September 2010).

Pretty long – opens out on the finish. But it's not a knocker-off-of-socks and has rather more classic Cheval character than some recent vintages. It's really quite subtle – but then there's no over-the-top ripeness, which is a relief. Rather contained and pretty. The challenge on the right bank after all was to keep it all in check ... (compared with the left bank, which could wallow more in the extra ripeness). Certainly not that sweet.

There are a number of fascinating and complicated issues here that will take us the remainder of the book to explore, but it seems to me that there is a notion of "experiential understanding" in play here that has important connections to the nature of aesthetic value and helps to identify the object of appreciation and the type and strength of normative demands inherent in our descriptions and evaluations of wine.

Something of this notion of understanding is nicely captured by Frank Sibley (2001), who contends that metaphors can be apt, appropriate or true in so far as they allow us better to understand and hence to appreciate the objects to which they apply. This notion of understanding is explained in terms of "seeing the point" of the metaphor, where "seeing the point" is partly an experiential – but also imaginative – phenomenon. This allows us, he claims, some amount of imaginative flexibility in the deployment of metaphors along certain dimensions and within certain parameters. The tannic texture of a wine, for example, might be correctly described as like silk, or like cashmere, but (if these are appropriate) not like sandpaper or pebble-dash.

Sibley's point is that the objectivity of metaphors is guaranteed by how well they allow us to understand the object to which they are applied, and this notion of understanding is partly experiential, depending on the idea that I "see the point" of describing the object in just that way; I taste and smell the wine under the description provided, in a way that *makes sense* of the object, just as the example from Robinson cited above illustrates.[6]

Now these notions of "understanding", "seeing the point", and "making sense of the object" are at this stage still relatively obscure, and we need now to expend a lot of energy in trying to pin them down, to make them clearer, in order to see whether they can help support the objectivity of wine tasting against the tyranny of personal prejudice and subjective idiosyncrasies that might seem to threaten it. In particular, we shall need them to help give some answer to the question that has been emerging from the considerations of Chapter 1: what exactly is the object of appreciation when we critically taste and assess a wine?

---

6. "There are of course no limits to the flights into those wildly exotic, exuberant, and flamboyant descriptions possible, and so often and easily ridiculed as pretentious, in the lucubrations of some who talk about food, wine, and perfumes ... When in ordinary discourse people bother, as specialists on wine, tea, food, and perfumes have to, to describe tastes and smells fully or carefully, what they say can sound as normal and unpretentious, and as appropriate, vivid, and accurate, as does the language of poets, novelists, or critics describing nature or artefacts" (Sibley 2001: 235–7).

Is it an ordinary, everyday, physical object in the external world, as common sense suggests, or is it rather an imaginative, interpretive, experiential object that somehow arises out of physical reality?

3

The Case for Objectivity I

Realism, Pluralism and Expertise

Senses of "subjective" and "objective"

We have so far seen that at least some of the judgments we make about wine, some of the words we use to describe it – including certain metaphors and evaluations – and some of our experiences of it, are firmly tethered to properties that we can with confidence say are really *in* the wine. They are there to be detected, independent of us, and hence have some claim to be "objective". We also touched on the idea that our judgements about wine may be grounded as much in certain conventions, norms and consensus among experts as in the perceptible properties of the wine. In this and the following chapter we need to look much more closely at the relations between all of these elements, for "subjectivity" and "objectivity" are extremely slippery notions, not merely in everyday usage, but also in philosophical parlance. Many different things can be meant by them, and just what it is that renders a particular realm of discourse and judgement objective or subjective is a matter of deep dispute among philosophers. So we shall need to tread very carefully in this treacherous terrain, and it's therefore important to begin with a brief and relatively simple overview of the territory.

All knowledge of the world that is attained through our sense perception is obviously subjective in the harmless sense that we thereby come to know the world through our subjective experiences of it; harmless because by itself this does not preclude the objectivity of our judgements concerning the external world. If I bump into a lamp post I will become aware of this object through the physical force that interacts with my body in the sense of touch, the pain that seeps through my forehead, and, when I've opened my dazed eyes, the sight of the lamp post before me. These are as good indications as any that there really is a lamp post before me. My judgement "there is a lamp post in front of me" will be objective because it is made true by the fact that there really is a lamp post there. I will therefore expect others to agree with me and to feel a similar pain to mine if they too bump into the lamp post.

When used to qualify our judgements about the external world, therefore, the charge of "subjectivity" acquires more bite, suggesting that our claims about external reality are mistaken, for they are merely about ourselves, about our own experiences, and have no valid application to how reality really is. The echoes of such a view were heard in Chapter 1: the view that the tastes and smells we experience when imbibing wine are not really in the wine, but in us; or if they are in the wine we can have no way of knowing this, for all of our knowledge consists only of our own subjective experiences.

Judgements of a wine's tastes and smells, on this view, would be subjective either in the sense that they are not true or false for they are not judgements about matters of fact at all, or they are about matters of fact, but merely facts about our own experiences. For the sake of convenience, let's call the first view "strong subjectivism", and the second view "weak subjectivism". According to strong subjectivism, our statements, which purport to be about objects, are not best understood in this way at all; rather, they should perhaps be understood as mere expressions of subjective experience. Such expressions have nothing to do with truth or falsity. If you say "ouch" when you bump into a lamp post, this is an *expression of* a subjective state of pain, but it is not a *statement about* the world as such, not even about your own psychological or experiential states. It is not a *judgement* that can be true or false, although naturally it is a true fact about you that you feel pain. Thus, strong subjectivism claims that our statements in some domain of discourse are not truth-apt.

According to weak subjectivism, our judgements in some domain should be understood as statements about our own subjective states, and as such they would be truth-apt. Compare the expression "ouch", which is not a statement about anything, to the proposition "I am in pain". This latter statement is about something, about some fact, and hence it can be true or false, even though the fact is a fact about my own inner, subjective states, rather than objects in the world.

On either reading of the subjectivity claim the implications are that nobody's assessment of wine is better or more correct than anybody else's, either because the statements are not "truth-apt" at all, but merely expressions of personal preference, or because all such statements are true if they are sincere reports about our own inner states. Things here really are just a matter of taste. According to strong subjectivism, for example, if you say that the Barbera d'Alba is unbalanced, too acidic, inelegant, you will not really be making a truth-apt statement about the wine, or even about your own experience of it. On the weak subjectivist's view, if you think the wine is unbalanced then you are right, if this is how it tastes to you, and if I think the opposite I too will be right if this is how it tastes to me. But notice that in this case we begin to lose our grip on the notions of "truth" and "right", because in fact we are talking about very different things. You are talking about your subjective experiences of the wine, and I am talking about mine. So although it looks like we are disagreeing about *the wine*, in fact we are not disagreeing about anything at all.

Are our judgements of wine subjective in either of these senses? It seems that there are many good reasons to think not, some of which were outlined in Chapter 2. At least for many of the descriptive judgements we make about the tastes and smells of wine, some measure of objectivity appears to be secured by empirical facts about wine. The Sancerre really smells herbaceous; the Chablis really tastes sharply acidic and smells minerally. Perhaps things become a little murkier when we begin using imaginative metaphors, and evaluating wines as good or bad. However, note that for all the scepticism frequently directed at the wine world and the claims of expertise, any serious reflection on our practices of wine production, drinking, conversation, criticism and appreciation will reveal that they heavily presuppose some level of objectivity.

If taste were wholly subjective, for example, there would be little point in trying to talk about wine with others, writing about wines in newspapers, putting tasting notes on wine labels, or communicating one's experiences in the hope of sharing them. It would not make much sense to suggest that someone try a wine in order to taste the flavours one took oneself as having detected, nor to think that you might have missed something in a wine, nor to worry that, lacking experience, you might fail to appreciate a fine wine at dinner. It would be pointless to attempt to cultivate or educate or improve one's palate, or to think it possible that one could learn about or come to a better understanding of wines. There would be no legitimate place for ranking systems, competitions or Master of Wine courses, and it would make a complete nonsense of wine production, pricing and a market firmly established on the assumption that wines possess certain qualities and that some wines just are better, and hence justifiably more expensive, than others.

Now of course, economic factors might all be a big swindle, and there is indeed some room for cynicism about the mechanisms of the wine market, and despair about the stratospheric prices of some fine wines. But, as in the art market, absurdly high prices do not entail that there is no good or better art, merely that some people are prepared to pay insanely high prices to procure it. The defender of objectivity will, further, point to the apparently widespread agreement about which wines are indisputably great and will emphasize the common conventions and norms that exist to frame and shape our wine judgements and ensure both standards of wine quality and of expertise.

In short, the existence of all of these features so integral to the nature of wine production, and our wine drinking practices, place a heavy burden of proof on those who would claim there are no objective facts about wine's values to ground them.

We must, however, be wary of making the defender of subjectivity into a straw man. Presumably, few individuals who enjoy wine, who have endeavoured to learn a little about it and who have thought even minimally about the nature of their appreciation would allow that there is literally nothing to the claims that many of our taste and smell experiences can accurately represent properties in the wine, and that these can also be discovered and appreciated by others. But they may object that such an allowance falls short of admitting into the realm of objectivity outlandish flights of metaphorical fancy, or perhaps even basic evaluative judgements such as "this Soave is good", "the Chianti is lacking finesse", or "that Primitivo is worse than this one".

They will point to the subjective features of our taste and smell experiences garnered in Chapter 1, the ineliminability of subjective preference in the assessment of wine quality, and the looseness and freedom with which language can be employed to express and describe our interaction with wine. Focusing on individual differences, they will emphasize the existence of supertasters as an indication that we are subject to different physical thresholds of sensitivity and discrimination, and that we therefore inhabit different taste worlds; and they will highlight research suggesting that taste – in the sense of perceptual ability as well as preference – varies culturally:

> Italians are generally more tolerant of bitterness, Americans of sweetness, Germans of sulphur dioxide, the French of tannins, and the British of decrepitude in their wines, while Australians tend to be particularly sensitive to mercaptans and most Americans view herbaceousness as a fault rather than a characteristic.   (Robinson 1999: 271)

Subjectivists will further stress the widespread *disagreement* that seems to prevail in many matters of taste, highlighting research apparently demonstrating that even experts are not particularly good at blind identifications of wines, and focusing on particular cases of disagreement even among supposed experts, such as the famous dispute between Jancis Robinson and Robert Parker over the quality of Château Pavie 2003. They may in this light attempt to explain away the conventions and bogus norms that underpin our current wine practices and faith in expertise by appealing to any number of different factors, such as vested economic interests, market forces, or entrenched sociocultural elitism, personal prejudice and class preferences. And they will find ready examples of this in cases such as the famous 1976 California versus France blind tasting event, in which the former significantly outscored the latter, which they have continued to do in repeated events (Ashenfelter *et al.* 2008).

Both sides of the objectivity/subjectivity debate seem to have strong intuitions and some evidence on their side, so how are we to decide? It would be helpful to begin by looking at the general nature of our evaluative judgements, which has been a fertile ground for philosophers to explore the various possible positions lying between the two rather extreme and unsubtle poles I have just sketched. In particular, many philosophers have appealed to the nature of aesthetic judgement to try to pin down the objectivity of our taste judgements – a natural analogue intimated by the use of the word "taste" to describe aesthetic and gustatory preferences alike – and the model for all such theories is that proposed by David Hume in his famous essay "Of the Standard of Taste".[1]

Hume's standard of taste

Hume's starting point is this tension between the pull to subjectivity on the one hand, and the pull to objectivity on the other.

---

1. See for example Sweeney (2008). The word "taste" is often used to refer to both the perceptual capacity of taste, and the notion of personal preference/ liking, as in "I like that, it is to my taste". The overlap in meanings, I think, stems from the old idea that aesthetic judgements were simple judgements of preference, like mere gustatory sensations, and so had no more objectivity than these. Hence the expression: "it's *just* a matter of taste".

He notes that aesthetic judgement is subject to a quite striking paradox. On the one hand, he says, "The great variety of Taste, as well as of opinion, which prevails in the world, is too obvious not to have fallen under every one's observation" (§1). The obvious explanation of this is that aesthetic judgements are merely subjective in the sense that they are simply reports about, or expressions of, one's own unique subjective experiences, what Hume calls "sentiments". Beauty really is just in the eye of the beholder. As such, all sentiments are equally valid or right, because:

> no sentiment represents what is really in the object. It only marks a certain conformity or relation between the object and the organs or faculties of the mind; and if that conformity did not really exist, the sentiment could never possibly have being. (§7)

On the other hand, however, Hume observes that there is universal agreement that some artworks are better than others, and hence that certain aesthetic judgements about them can be right or wrong. The two features of aesthetic judgement clearly appear to be incompatible. To resolve this paradox, Hume aims to demonstrate how aesthetic taste can be in some sense subjective and yet our judgements of taste deemed correct or incorrect, that is, objective and truth-apt. Hume's ingenious solution depends on pursuing an analogy with our colour discriminations.

The idea is this. Colours are subjective in that they depend on us for their perception. They are secondary, response-dependent properties, as we saw in Chapter 1. But they correspond in a causal way to real physical properties in the external world – wavelengths of light, various refractive and reflective properties of surfaces, the physical constitution of our visual processing system – and it is the way this information is processed by us that anchors the application of colour terms to objects. The objectivity of our colour judgements is thus secured by a twofold combination: on the one hand by reference to these *real properties* in the world and their *real causal interaction* with us, but on the other hand by *intersubjective agreement* in the way that this information is "subjectively" processed. That is, the norm for colour judgements is established by reference to the standard perceptual capacities of the majority – thus excluding, for example, the colour-blind – and to standard conditions for colour discrimination, such as being viewed in normal daylight, and not in a darkened room through tinted glasses.

Philosophers thus generally analyse colour judgements in the following manner:

X is red if and only if X appears red to a "normal" observer under "standard observation conditions".

Thus, these conditions allow us to distinguish right from wrong colour judgements and to establish the conditions for objective judgements concerning them, even though colours depend on the contingent fact that most human beings happen to be wired up to the world in just this way, and even though the deployment of colour concepts depends on our *subjective* colour experiences. Disagreement will always, therefore, be put down to a fault in the perceptual conditions of the perceiver, or the conditions of observation, and there will be empirical methods – at least in principle – for explaining and resolving any disagreements.

An important question, among many, that such an account raises is whether objectivity is established by mere agreement, something many philosophers would wish to avoid. For it is desirable to allow in most cases that the majority may, for whatever reason, be wrong. The truth and objectivity of judgements concerning the flatness of the earth, for instance, would not be secured by a majority belief in its flatness. Objectivity is not mere majority, although objectivity will be a good explanation of why there is, for any realm of judgement, widespread agreement.

Happily, we can make sense of this when considering colours. Imagine that almost all normally sighted colour perceivers vanished from the earth, leaving only the colour-blind behind and just one normally sighted person. Would the colour judgements of the lonely soul left behind be rendered false by reference to the colour-blind majority? Arguably not, for the colours are still there to be perceived even if the majority cannot, as it happens, perceive them. So although our standard for objective colour judgements is established relative to intersubjective agreement, this objectivity is not *reducible to* mere agreement. The right causal conditions must also be in place, and these conditions exist objectively in so far as they would be there to inform perception even if no one actually went about perceiving them.

Hume thus holds that the best explanation of aesthetic agreement – the objective intuition – is to hold that there is some sort of causal link between us and the objects that are "fitted by nature" to cause in us the *subjective* experiences that we express in our aesthetic judgements, and which alert us to the presence of the aesthetic properties in the object that we thereby label with our judgements. Aesthetic properties, that is, depend for their existence and perception on us and our interaction with real properties in the world. But they are no less real or objective for that.

Are aesthetic judgements just like colour judgements in all of these respects? Not quite, and the differences are salient for understanding whether this model for objectivity can be applied to wine tasting.

Unlike colours, Hume claims that aesthetic qualities are much subtler, finer and more difficult to perceive, and the "organ" of the mind that perceives them is fragile and sensitive, "of a very tender and delicate nature" that is prone to hindrance and disruption. For this reason we require the external conditions for perception to be perfect, but we must also be perfectly equipped *internally* to be properly attuned to perceiving these qualities. We must, for instance, be in the right frame of mind and pay "due attention to the object" (§10).

This gives rise to a further significant difference. Because, Hume says, aesthetic qualities are difficult to perceive in the ways outlined, there may be very few people fitted to discern them. Moreover, this is not just a case of nature, but of nurture: one's perceptual faculties can be trained, educated and improved in a number of ways. This is a crucial point. Our colour discrimination is just a brute causal fact about how most people react to certain properties in the world. We do not train people to *see* colours, or provide *reasons* for making our colour judgements, and although we have to learn to name colours, this naming does not affect our actual ability to detect them as such. In contrast, our aesthetic discriminations are partly perceptual, but they also depend partly on various background *non-perceptual factors* that actually affect our perception, such as practice and experience in comparison, freedom from prejudice and "delicacy of sentiment" (§23).

So, whereas the objectivity of colour judgements depends on how the majority of human beings happen to physically interact with features of the external world, the objectivity of aesthetic judgements is a little more precarious, requiring the right kind of delicate interaction with the external world that is the preserve of the few, namely, the expert critics: "the joint verdict of such, wherever they are to be found, is the true standard of taste and beauty" (*ibid.*).

In part, then, Hume's account of aesthetic objectivity depends on what philosophers refer to as an *ideal observer* theory. Colour judgements depend on "normal" perceivers, but the detection of aesthetic value requires reference to a restricted class of "ideal" observers. And it partially depends, in addition, on the consensus of these observers, due to the sensitive, error-prone and subtle nature of aesthetic perception. Disagreements, in other words, may be difficult to resolve, a lot can go wrong, and there may be wide variation in the abilities of critics that Hume lists as essential to their expertise. The consensus of ideal critics, therefore, is required to ensure that we get the right verdict.

Whatever the plausibility of Hume's account of the objectivity of aesthetic judgements, can we draw from it a plausible account of the objectivity of our "taste" judgements about wine? Do such judgements resemble our colour discriminations, our aesthetic assessments (as Hume outlines them), some combination of the two, or neither? To spoil the denouement somewhat, I will eventually argue that much of Hume's theory can be broadly applied to wine judgements – which is why I have spent so much time outlining it – although things are a little more complicated than Hume's account suggests, particularly when it come to accounting for and resolving disagreements in judgement among experts and the role of evaluation in such judgements.

Before doing this, however, we should first examine one of the most recent, and most robust, philosophical defences of the objectivity of wine tasting: that provided by Barry Smith (2007b). This will provide a perfect point of departure for developing a response to the central problems arising from Smith's and Hume's accounts.

Realism and pluralism

Smith defends what he calls a *realist* position about tastes; namely, the idea that although our judgements of taste are "response-dependent" in that like colours they depend on subjective responses, the properties to which our judgements refer – properties such as

balance, suppleness, finesse – are *really* in the wine, objective features of it to which we have access through our taste and smell
experiences, given the right conditions. As such, realism allows us
to make the crucial distinction between how things seem to us
and how they really are. We can, in other words, get things wrong
about the real properties of the wine. This is a crucial feature of
any realist/objectivist position, for subjectivism – as we saw earlier
– simply does not allow for any such distinction: how a thing tastes
to us just is its taste. As Hume says, on such a view, "all sentiment
is right" for there is nothing in the world to which it refers.

One of Smith's primary arguments for realism is that it provides
the best explanation of our current practices of talking about and
judging wine, practices such as those listed at the beginning of
this chapter. Before looking in more detail at Smith's arguments,
it will be helpful to see how it is distinct from a contending objectivist view that can be seen as having its roots in a Humean-style
account of value, but which Smith is concerned to reject.[2]

One might, for example, hold that the objectivity of taste consists *merely* in *intersubjective agreement* among some group of individuals; it does not hold in virtue of discovering properties such
as balance or finesse really in the wine. A powerful objection to
this view is that it fails to explain why there is such agreement
at all, and fails to explain why "we draw one another's attention
to aspects of a wine's taste, and value the accuracy and precision
with which people do this" (Smith 2007b: 61). But this objection

---

2. Smith himself attributes such a view to Deroy (2007).

can be answered in the following way, by appealing to what philosophers call "*dispositional properties*". Properties such as balance or finesse are not as such genuine properties of a wine, but are just dispositions of the chemical properties that *are really in* the wine to produce certain pleasurable tastes in "normal perceivers". Normal perceivers are identified as those who are, in the relevant way, statistically normal for some population of tasters, and what counts as normal may itself be a cultural matter (66–7).

Smith's first objection to this view is that it gives us a misguided way of identifying and valuing the taste of wine, for we don't make our judgements based on reflection about how some statistically normal tasters would react to some set of chemicals in the wine. A better explanation of why we taste what we do is simply to attribute those tastes to the wine itself (63). His second objection is that in lieu of any obvious way of restricting whose dispositions count, and which interactions are the right ones, any given wine would have to be attributed a proliferation of often incompatible tastes.

Now one might think that Smith is being a little unfair on the dispositionalist here. After all, one can attempt to demarcate whose dispositions count, as Hume himself did, by appealing to the notion of the "ideal" taster, the expert, and specifying the right conditions for tasting (cf. Deroy 2007: 120). But now we fall back on the problem that Hume recognized: how do we non-arbitrarily identify the right critics? That is, how do we circumscribe the right set of responses except by appealing to that set which accurately detects the tastes of the wine? But such an appeal will simply give rise to a circular account: what properties does the wine possess? Those that are detected by the experts. How do we identify the experts? They are those people who detect those properties in the wine.

Hume himself was sanguine about this problem, expecting that our common-sense practices and procedures of decision, observation and argument would allow us to spot the true critics, partly because we can expect that their judgements will converge over time, which is a sure sign of objectivity. Naturally, it must be remembered that Hume was talking about art criticism rather than wine criticism, but why not think the same principles apply? Smith's telling point, however, is that any such evidence we find in favour of the existence of expertise, such as a convergence in judgements, will then be best explained not circularly and hence uninformatively in terms of some set of dispositions, but rather by appeal to the actual, real existence of those properties in the wine.

Smith's main argument for realism is, as I noted above, essentially that our current practices of judgement presuppose it, and it is the best explanation of such practices. These include essential features of our wine tasting experience such as the distinction we readily make between how a wine appears to taste and how it really tastes. If we were only describing our subjective experiences then all the judgements we purport to make about wine would be literally false. We avoid pronouncing on the qualities of a wine if suffering a bout of nausea, and we avoid ruining a decent claret by heating it in the microwave. We say that there are qualities to be found in the wine, to be experienced, and we take seriously the accusation that we might have missed something in the wine. Moreover, we think it important to analyse a fine wine with the concentration it deserves, paying attention to the inter- actions and relationships between its smells and tastes, and we talk of wines as rewarding (or not) such attention in virtue of the complex qualities that are there to be detected and understood.

As such, it makes sense to distinguish the analytic experiences of experts from non-experts, for only the former are trying to *make sense* of the taste and smell experiences as really belong- ing to the wine, to detect just what sort of fruit they can smell in the concentrated first nose, whether it is ripe or overripe, and whether it is present also on the palate; to *understand* whether and how the winemaker has succeeded in balancing the young, harsh wood tannins, against the fruit's natural acidity. Is there enough alcohol and extract to give the wine body, or has the rich, con- centrated nose that promised a full and complex wine deceived, belying the tough tannins, and unbalanced, light-bodied nature of a rough and overly alcoholic wine?[3] These are questions and forms of attention that shape the way in which an expert tastes, that shape the nature of her taste and smell experiences, and that underpin the idea that the aim of such tasting is to detect the tastes and smells that are really there in the wine to be detected.

---

3. A good recent example of these kinds of questions and patterns of attention in action can be found in the debates about the merits of the 2009 vintage of Right Bank Bordeaux.

Here for example is Robert Parker's assessment of the 2009
L'Eglise Clinet:

> This dense purplecolored 2009 (which achieved 14.5%
> natural alcohol) is extremely powerful, but that power is
> concealed beneath a mountain of glycerin, fruit, concen-
> tration, and body. The purity and richness are off the
> charts, and the silkiness of the tannins is ethereal. This
> extraordinary wine possesses extremely high levels of
> tannin, but according to Durantou, they have almost dis-
> appeared because of the wine's amazing depth and rich-
> ness.   (*Wine Advocate*, April 2010)

As Smith emphasizes, therefore, tasting is not a passive experience, but requires attention, concentration and training, and
he is clearly right about this, as anybody who has ever tried to
taste wine in the analytical way required to *judge* it will know.
The judging is essentially experiential but not reducible to *simple*
sensory experience, the unmediated "feeling" of taste and smell
sensations. The experiences, that is to say, are *cognitively penetrable*,
as I suggested in Chapter 1. Expertise affects *what* one perceptually
experiences, in virtue of the various assumptions and expectations
that form the background framework that structures one's tasting.
Experienced tasters will learn more from their sensations about
the nature of the wine than non-experienced tasters, and blind
tasting with knowledge will allow one to experience a jumble of
different chemical compounds as possessing a structure that can

be appreciated and understood. As such, as we noted earlier, only fine wines will, in virtue of their complexity, reward the attention we pay to them – the better the quality of the wine, the better the quality of the experience of drinking it.

Arguably the greatest difficulty facing this kind of account is explaining disagreement in judgements, particularly among experts, for, after all, if tastes are really in the wine, we should expect some sort of convergence in judgement among the experts. Part of a response to this would be to play down the extent of these disagreements. However, just how much agreement or disagreement there is among experts is in part an empirical claim, and to that extent clear evidence on one side or another is difficult to procure. A more satisfying philosophical response is to point to the *nature* of perceived disagreements and try to explain them away. This, in effect, is Smith's strategy.

Taking his cue from one of Hume's examples, the first part of Smith's response consists in defending the idea that wines may contain many different tastes; that is, he supports *pluralism* about tastes. Certain apparent disagreements may then be resolved by pointing out that different judgers are sensitive to different tastes in the wine. You say the Savennières smells of ripe apples; I say it smells of under-ripe pears. We both may be right, for the wine may indeed possess both smells, neither of which is incompatible with the other. Here, therefore, there is in fact no genuine conflict.

The second part of Smith's response consists in making a distinction – as we can in the case of judging art – between subjective preferences and real wine quality, a distinction that readily follows from his realist account and is a crucial piece of the objectivist's toolkit.

If a wine offers a perfectly balanced expression of the uniqueness of its *terroir* and the lush lychee taste typical of the Gewürztraminer varietal, this may redound to the winemaker's credit and constitute the reason for the critic's judgement that it is a good wine; whether the critic *likes* it, however, is another matter entirely: or not quite entirely, as we shall see later. But it is perfectly possible, and indeed not at all unusual, for experts to judge as to the qualities of wines that are not to their personal taste. I may hate the taste and smell of lychees and yet appreciate the Gewürztraminer's harmony and finesse. Furthermore, sometimes, in some contexts, I may prefer a simple, rough table wine to a complex fine wine, even while acknowledging that the latter is *objectively* better and more interesting, just as I may at times prefer to listen to Mozart rather than Schoenberg, or read Asterix comics rather than Proust, without this entailing anything about the respective objective value I attribute to each.

We can see why, in this light, Smith claims that many apparent disagreements between experts are actually *blameless*, for they may come down to implicit, and at times unrecognized, differences between individual preferences that "may leave untouched an underlying agreement about the properties … of the wine" (2007b: 71). We might both agree that the 2002 Côte-Rôtie "La Turque" has a powerful, spicy nose, chocolate and tar undertones, masses of ripe dark fruit on the palate, chunky yet soft tannins, is not overly oaked, and is tightly structured and with high alcohol.

My score of 15/20 reflects the fact that, although an excellent wine, I prefer rather more austere Côte-Rôties, which, I feel, better express a certain finesse and nerviness that capture certain elements of the *terroir* that are worth highlighting, and that avoid the tendency to become Parker-like "blockbuster" caricatures to which recent Côte-Rôties are prone. Your score of 18/20, on the other hand, reflects a preference for, and appreciation of, the big, fruity, alcoholic and sweet characteristics of which such wines are uniquely capable. Here, the realist says, disagreement is not about the taste properties really possessed by the wine, but merely about subjective preferences.

The relativist threat

As was the case with Hume's account, I have spent time sketching Smith's realist position because there is clearly so much about it that is plausible, insightful and worth preserving. However, there are some challenges that must be faced and it is unclear that realism about tastes, as Smith conceives it, will survive unscathed. In order to meet them we'll eventually see that a new position will emerge that, I will contend, better accommodates some of the complexities of wine and its appreciation.

To recap, Smith argues that realism provides the best explanation of our practices and that this entails that we must be pluralist about tastes, as otherwise we would be forced to admit a "proliferation of tastes" that would undermine the fundamental realist idea that there is just one set of tastes in any given wine. The worry with Smith's stance is this: given that the properties we attribute to wine are "response-dependent", and given apparent variations in taste and the disagreements commonly attending our judgements, why shouldn't we allow that there may be more than one valid set of incompatible responses to a wine?

If one wanted to be a realist about taste and yet make this allowance, one would be forced then to attribute incompatible properties to the wine. But this looks metaphysically suspicious, for it would no longer make sense to think that there is just one *wine object* consisting of real tastes existing independently of what any particular taster detects. Rather, it seems we would be forced to hold the dispositionalist position that the wine object is just a bundle of *powers* to affect different tasters in various ways. As we saw, one could attempt to limit the damage by stipulating just one set of tasters as the ideal set of experts, but it is not obvious that there is a non-question-begging way of doing this, that there is sufficient agreement to allow it, or that all apparent disagreements can in principle be resolved, which is what such a view would require.

An alternative position arising from these concerns is that provided by the *relativist*, who holds that truth is relative to different perspectives or tastes. Note that the relativist too thinks our judgements about wine may have some claim to objectivity – perhaps in many of the same ways as supported by the realist – but they will hold that there may be more than one set of right, and yet incompatible, judgements. Different experts disagreeing about a particular wine may, that is, both be right. According to the relativist, there may be blameless disagreements about at least some of the properties attributed to a wine, where these cannot always be accounted for, as Smith holds, merely in terms of pluralism and different subjective preferences about the same objective properties.

In short, the question now at issue can be seen like this: which account, realist or relativist, provides the best explanation of our wine tasting practices, and in particular of disagreements in judgement among experts? Or is there perhaps a third way between these two positions? Trying to answer these questions will now take us deeper into the heart of our appreciation of wine.

4

The Case for Objectivity II
Relativism, Evaluation and Disagreement

Categories and conventions

The best place to begin is with a closer examination of some of the issues alighted on in the second chapter concerning the nature and role of conventions in establishing the various norms for wine language and judgement, and the role of expertise therein.

The first thing that really needs to be emphasized here, a theme we have touched on already at various points, is that what we perceive and experience in wine is not anchored solely in basic "unmediated" or "un-interpreted" perceptual properties – the bare sensations – of taste and smell. For it can be contoured and coloured by a range of background factors, including education, knowledge, culture, imagination, categorization, comparison, intention and so on. That is, our taste and smell experiences of wine are to some degree *cognitively penetrable*, as we noted in Chapter 1. What we think, know and imagine can affect what we pay attention to and focus on, what we expect to taste, what we taste, and even our liking for what we taste. We need now to assess the respects in which this is so, and try to locate the thresholds governing such penetration. Again, the model we can use is taken from the realm of aesthetic judgement and appreciation.

In a now classic paper, the philosopher Kendall Walton (1970) famously demonstrated that what aesthetic properties a work of art is *perceived to have* depends on which of its non-aesthetic properties are *standard*, *variable* and *contra-standard* relative to the categories in which it is perceived. So, for example, relative to the category "painting", flatness will be a standard feature, variable features will include the particular colours, shapes and patterns actually painted, and contra-standard features will include the presence of any features that tend to exclude a particular work from that category, such as, in the case of painting, possessing three-dimensional figures or moving parts.

Now Walton examines how this categorization affects our aesthetic judgements of artworks by asking us to imagine a society that does not have the medium of painting as such. Instead, they have a kind of work of art called "*guernicas*", which are like Picasso's picture *Guernica* but done in various bas-relief dimensions. They have the same colours and shapes of *Guernica* but the surfaces are moulded to protrude from the wall like relief maps of terrain. So relative to the category "*guernica*", flatness would be a variable (and perhaps even contra-standard) feature rather than a standard feature. Some *guernicas* have rolling surfaces, others are sharp and jagged, others relatively flat and so on. Now in this society, relative to the category "*guernica*", Picasso's *Guernica* would be a perfectly flat *guernica* rather than a painting. Its flatness is *variable* and the figures on its surface are *standard* relative to the category *guernica*. Thus, although its flatness is standard for us, it is variable for them, and the figures depicted are variable for us, but standard for them.

The first crucial point is this: the different categories against which we perceive Picasso's picture make for profound differences in our aesthetic reactions to it. To us, relative to our category "painting", *Guernica* seems "violent, dynamic, vital, disturbing", but in the society where "*guernica*" is itself a category, relative to this category Picasso's *Guernica* may seem, in contrast, for example, cold, stark, lifeless, and perhaps bland or dull. For this society, what is expressive and different about Picasso's picture is its flatness, while its actual design and colour patches are insignificant since they are standard. So, how we *perceive* and what we *perceive* in an artwork are affected by the category relative to which we perceive it.

The second crucial claim of Walton's paper is this. In some cases it is *correct* to perceive a work in certain categories, and *incorrect* to perceive it in others. It is correct to perceive Picasso's picture in the category "painting", for example, rather than the category "novel". How do we determine the correct categories in which to perceive any given work? Walton acknowledges that this is a tricky question, but he cites the following four conditions as relevant to determining this:

- the presence in the work of a relatively large number of features standard with respect to the relevant category;
- the fact that the work appears "better" when perceived in the relevant category;
- the fact that the maker intended for it to be so perceived in this category;
- that the category is well established and recognized by the society in which the work was produced.

In short, I think that a proper, appropriate understanding and appreciation of wine, and hence the objectivity of the judgements and assessments grounded therein, is category-relative in a directly analogous way. Here is a brief list of some of the categories that are operative in the wine world and that govern its various practices of production, assessment, and ranking:

- *Grape varieties*: chardonnay, pinot noir, and so on.
- *Geography*: country, region, local *terroir*, and so on.
- *Intentions*: owner, producer, *negociant*, and so on.
- *Age/maturity/vintage*: young, old, good/bad vintage, and so on.
- *Style* (linked with *intention*): General – red, white, sparkling (perhaps also New World, Old World). Specific – dry, fruity, sweet, full-bodied, and so on.
- *Quality* (linked with *intention*): *Grand Cru*, *Premier Cru*, fine wine, table wine, and so on.

Just as in the case of art, there are degrees of specificity and generality to which wine categorization is subject, some of these categories overlap, and there are many complex variables that affect the categorization and category-relative judgements of any given wine. Where art-category judgements often involve complex, uncertain and shifting "institutional" boundaries and values, and require reference to often vague or unknown artistic intentions, the *correct* categories within which to assess wine have generally been – until quite recently – relatively stable, subject to relatively rigid institutionalized classification systems, and well-established varietal and geographic features and appellations. Moreover, the intentions of winemakers are often relatively clear and accessible and the relevant valuable characteristics of wines that are to be appreciated are in many cases written on the labels themselves.

Of course, it is important not to stress these differences too much. The various factors operating in the categories governing the production and ranking of Burgundy wines, for instance, are well known for their fiendish, at times almost impenetrable, complexity. There are also good reasons to think that some wine categories and styles are in a state of flux, especially in, but certainly not restricted to, the New World areas where producers are constantly experimenting with different varietals and combinations, introducing new technologies and in general exploring new wine styles. What have traditionally been thought the typical characteristics of a Cabernet Sauvignon, Merlot or Chenin Blanc, for example, have been thrown into question, and at times into some confusion, by the proliferation of wine styles in a now vast and diverse global wine market. Compare the consumer contempt for the simple fruit-friendly New World Merlot so disparaged in the film *Sideways* with the glorious, elegant and complex manifestation of Merlot in a Château Pétrus or La Conseillante.

There can be little doubt that the changing face of wine styles poses challenges for experts by threatening both the implicit norms that guide their expectations and judgements, and the very idea that there are right and wrong categories at all. We shall return below to the implications for objectivity of these shifting categorial sands. For the moment it will suffice to note that these complexities should not be used to mask the various reliable ways in which category-relative judgements can, and have, grounded the objectivity of wine tasting.

Here are some examples of category-relative judgements in action. Relative to the varietal category "chardonnay", a drinker familiar only with what might be called old-style Australian chardonnays − big, intense, very alcoholic, fruit-driven wines with strong oaky aromas − may well be likely to perceive, and hence describe, a white Meursault from Burgundy as "austere" or "reserved". However, when compared to a Chablis (also a chardonnay-based wine) it will be seen that the Meursault is not really austere at all; rather, it might be better described as soft, gentle, buttery or subtle in comparison to the classic flintiness, minerality and high acidity that ground a description such as austere for Chablis. Standard perceptible properties for the relatively specific "Chablis" category will include high acidity on the palate, a certain minerality, and hint of crisp citrus on the nose;

variable properties might include, for instance, the specific level of acidity, the type of the citrus detected and so on.

In comparison to a typical Chablis, a Pinot Noir from New Zealand may be perceived and described as big or beefy, but relative to other wines within the category "red wine", it may not be so adequately characterized. More specifically, a subtle red from St-Joseph in the Rhône, lacking in the characteristic big, beefy, tannic intensity typical of – that is, a standard feature of – the "Rhône Syrah" category, may properly be described as feminine and delicate relative to this category. Next to a typical red Burgundy, however – with their more restrained, cooler, subtle and delicate Pinot Noir aromas and less tannic structure – it may no longer appear so delicate or feminine, and would not be accurately assessed as such.

At a broader level, in the category "red wine", while the typical Burgundy style might aptly be described as feminine, there will of course be many Burgundies that are not suitably described as such, either because they fail to handle the difficult Pinot Noir grape, or because they aim for a different style altogether. To take a final example, relative to the category "Burgundy *grand cru*", a particular Clos de la Roche vintage may seem disappointing, intense but lacking in subtlety, brutal rather than refined, pedestrian rather than expressive. But relative to the generic category "Red Burgundy" it may still be judged a great wine, refined and subtle, sophisticated, elegant and expressive.

It is important to note that the broader and more general the categories – for example chardonnay, Californian, New World –

the less easy it may be to pinpoint standard and variable properties pertaining to them, an inevitable symptom of the greater variety of wines available and the large and rapid changes that have swept across the wine world over the past few decades. Standard properties for New World, for example, may once have been "big", "intense", "ripe fruit", "alcoholic", but, as I noted above, things are no longer so simple. In contrast, the more specific a category becomes, the clearer and narrower the range of its standard properties, and the more important its assessment in terms of variable and contra-standard properties will be. For example, high acidity, crisp clean "wet stones" on the nose may all be classed as standard properties for the relatively specific Chablis category, while variable properties will include, for instance, the presence and type of subtle citrus flavours, and within the Chablis category different vineyards will have their own styles that determine some of the standard and variable properties for them. These sorts of factors will crucially affect how we assess individual wines.

So, as we saw in Chapter 2, judgements that a wine is X must thus be understood to include an implicit "relative to this type or category", and wines can be judged as *typical* or not relative to the category in which they are being assessed. Such knowledge will govern the *way in which* we taste wine, the expectations and attention we bring to our appreciation and perception – we will look for features in the wine that we expect relative to categories against which it should be assessed – and how the wine tastes to us. We thus need some ability to make, as it were in our imaginations, comparisons with the right category when actually perceiving a particular wine, and the imagination too plays a central role in capturing our experiences in metaphors that make sense of the wine and guide the understanding of others. This requires experience and practice, and the possession of this background knowledge is just what marks the expert from the non-expert.

But this knowledge is not always worn on the sleeve, and more often than not it remains *implicit*. This is perhaps one reason why disagreements are so ready to arise in this area. Recall here our discussion from Chapter 2. If I say that the Chablis is austere this could be taken in a number of different ways. "Austere" relative to what? How austere exactly is it? If I'm talking to someone whom I recognize as knowing something about this style of wine, I can be understood to mean "austere even by the typical standards of Chablis". In contrast, if I am talking to a non-expert, or just someone relatively unfamiliar with the Chablis style, my aim may be to communicate that this Chablis is austere relative to most other types of white wine, whereas in fact by the standards of Chablis, this particular Chablis might not in fact be particularly austere at all.

It is perhaps important to remind ourselves at this juncture that the way in which expertise functions in the conventions of the wine world is not so different *in kind* from the way in which it functions in other domains, as I have remarked a number of times already (Chs 1 & 2; see also Origgi 2007: esp. 194–5).

Right and wrong categories

That's all very well, you might say, but why think that there are right and wrong categories against which to judge wine? Who decides these? To some extent, the right response to this worry is to boldly state that "nobody simply decides". These categories are established partly because they reflect obvious differences in geography and geology, in winemaking techniques and traditions, and, most importantly, different perceptual differences arising from different grape varieties. The various institutions and legal frameworks and appellation systems governing winemaking conventions throughout the world are ultimately founded simply on the fact that there are certain properties of grape and *terroir* that can give rise to certain valuable experiences in us. The establishment of these categories is thus not arbitrary, or *mere* convention, but depends in large part on the existence of certain physical properties of wine types and our physical propensities and thresholds involved in experiencing them.

In short, the existence of categories both reflects and ensures the manifestation of these remarkable features of fermented grapes. Judging wines relative to the right categories against which they should be assessed is important, ultimately, because it will – all things being equal – allow us to experience the greatest amount of the qualities, and to the highest degree, of which that grape variety, that *terroir*, that wine is capable. That is, if we were to appreciate and assess Californian chardonnays *in the same ways* as we appreciate and assess Chablis, if we were to try to *experience* them in the same ways, looking for the same values and qualities, we would end up doing a disservice to the wine and robbing ourselves of the qualities specific to that type or style of wine. It is for these reasons that we should be interested in the *existence* of right and wrong categories, and in *knowing* what they are when assessing any given wine.

The correctness of the descriptive judgements we make about wine are, as we have seen, based partly on direct, and in large part empirically testable, correlations between physical properties of the wine and the tastes and smells we perceive them as having. Where we employ metaphors to describe wine, our metaphors will be appropriate if they can be fully paraphrased in terms of non-metaphorical physical attributes of the wine, or if they are at least grounded in certain conventions that are commonly understood, accepted and used among the experts whose agreement in part supports the convention.

Now this kind of account of objectivity works well for a range of descriptive judgements dependent on stable descriptive categories. Some of these categories are centrally premised on *descriptive* geographical classifications, ranging from the general to the specific. A bottle of Chablis is a Chablis simply in virtue of being produced within the designated Chablis region, but these geographical categories ensure, at a basic general level, standard grape varieties and the manifestation of properties latent in them, leading one to expect a certain style of wine. Furthermore, many of these boundaries ensure certain standards of winemaking that allow, for instance, certain acid levels to be attained, or the addition of/avoidance of certain additives, or certain tech-niques of bottling and barrelling, and so on. This supports the stabilization of certain categories, such as what constitutes a *typical* Chablis.

When it comes to establishing the objectivity of wine *quality* however, the story becomes rather more complicated. Among the categories I listed are *evaluative classifications* of quality, ranging from those wines satisfying minimal quality standards, such as *vin de table*, through the levels of *cru bourgeois* and *premier cru* up to *grand cru* and equivalents. Thus, within the category "Chablis" are found both *premier cru* and *grand cru* appellations. These evaluative categories should reflect respective differences in the qualities of wine relative to them. The worry, however, is that different wines present different value qualities and serve different functions, and that categories are amenable to becoming so narrow that compari-son of quality across them becomes meaningless. The challenge is clearly formulated by Justin Weinberg, who argues that "it makes little sense to ask about the quality of wine. Generally, wines are incommensurable; that is, we cannot mark them as better or worse along a single scale" (2008: 263–4).

There is something to this worry. It doesn't seem to make any more sense to compare the *overall* quality of a red Hermitage to a Château d'Yquem, than it does to compare the overall quality of Monet's *Water Lilies* with one of Yves Klein's monochrome blue works, Edward Lear with Proust, or Schubert's *Schwanenge-sang* with John Cage's *4'33"*. Or perhaps, you might even think it would be like comparing across artistic genres – Joyce's *Ulysses* with, say, one of Bach's violin partitas. But I think Weinberg greatly overstates his case.

Of course, within a particular narrow evaluative category it may not be straightforward to say which of a range of *grand cru* wines will be better than another. Indeed, plausibly, there will often be no fact of the matter about this, and such fine-grained and specific judgements may well be partly a matter of taste, that is, personal preference. The choice between a Château Latour 1982 and Château Margaux 1982 may be in this respect as personal (indeed as incommensurable) as that between Beethoven's Ninth and Brahms's Second Violin Sonatas. However, it does not follow that there are not meaningful comparisons of quality to be made both within and across many of the categories governing appreciation.

In large part the hierarchy of evaluative categories is, I think, founded on types of value that wine can possess *qua* wine, which delineate the category "fine wine" and so assure, for instance, that a *vin de table* will generally not be as good (*qua* wine) as a *premier cru*. There is a range of agreed intrinsic values that mark out the superior from the inferior both between, and to some extent within, categories. What ultimately grounds the categories of quality is the ability of the best wines to manifest to the highest degree those intrinsic values of which wine *qua* wine is capable.

A fuller discussion of wine values must wait until Chapter 5, but it is helpful, I feel, to make the following important points before returning to discuss the objectivity of wine evaluations. Some of these values are expressive, and other prominent values include clarity, being without blemish, balance, intensity, complexity, and personality, distinctiveness or *terroir*. These are qualities of objects that we tend to value intrinsically, and they are not particular to wine, although, of course, the ways in which they are manifested in wine are particular to it. Complex objects are more interesting than non-complex objects, and the more complex it is the more the object rewards our attention. The more likely, too, it is to bring with it unexpected elements that surprise us, and being (pleasantly) surprised is itself a state that we value as the antithesis of monotony and boredom. Moreover, the ability to discriminate brings its own kind of pleasure. It takes effort, knowledge and trained perceptual and linguistic abilities to discern and enjoy the character of complex wines, wines that are aptly described using terms such as "subtle", "sophisticated", "refined".

This is an important point because the nature of such attention is itself complex: it involves perceptual awareness, concentration, skill, experience, imagination and all the cognitive resources necessary to understand and interpret the perceptible properties on offer, relative to all those categories and factors already mentioned. If such features are the hallmarks of aesthetic attention then wine can certainly be a rewarding aesthetic object. These are the values one will expect the best wines to have, in quantity and degree.

Of course, in certain contexts, relative to certain functions and interests, simplicity, for example, might be the sought-for value, and table wines best suited to deliver it. Yet such wine will not reward any efforts at sustained attention and discrimination, and nor does one drink such wine in order to experience these kinds of satisfaction. There is a time and place for such wines, just as there is a time and place for escapist literature and popular entertainment rather than the often demanding nature of high art. One is not always ready to sit down with Proust. But *qua* wines, these simple examples will lack, either completely or in terms of degree, those values against which judgements of quality are ultimately measured, that is, those values that fine wines are capable of possessing and which are valued intrinsically. Balance, complexity and intensity seem to me the *sine qua non* of wine quality.

However, we do not just regard complexity in wines as valuable, for as philosophers of art have for centuries recognized, beauty in objects is often partly a matter of discovering unity in variety. The balance and harmony achieved among a large array of different elements in objects is intrinsically rewarding, as well as being valued as an exemplification of the skill evident in accomplishing it. We naturally seek to make sense of the complex worlds of perceptual and intellectual discrimination, of the massive amount of information with which we are constantly bombarded, and no doubt our effort to seek, and pleasure in finding, intelligible patterns in the morass can be given a psycho-evolutionary explanation; but more on this later.

Granted the existence of such values, it is worth re-emphasizing the distinction, which many philosophers have commented on, between evaluation and preference. Judgements of fine wine not only need not correspond with what one (or the majority) happens to find pleasant (in a gustatory sense); indeed, judgement and gustatory pleasure may well conflict. One may discern the value qualities of a wine without straightforwardly *liking* them. Of course, ultimately the value that wines have is intrinsically connected to the pleasure they provide. It is to be expected that the pleasures of connoisseurs will thus generally match the wines they take to be the most valuable. But this does not entail that judgements of value are simply reducible to basic subjective, sensual, gustatory pleasures, for these will be influenced, moulded and modified by the norms and values that come to structure one's understanding and appreciation.

So, just as in other areas of aesthetic appreciation, judgements of the quality and value of wine are not reducible to, and may in principle even conflict with, mere judgements of personal taste. It makes perfect sense to say, for example, that "this Sauternes is well-balanced and complex", "this Sauternes is a great wine" or "Sauternes is superior to Beaumes-de-Venise" while personally disliking these styles of wine, sweet wines in general, and so on. This also accounts for the otherwise peculiar judgements that a wine smelling of something unpleasant, such as barnyard muck, cat's pee or wet dog, may nevertheless be valued, say, as an excellent wine partly *in virtue of* this very (distasteful) quality (see also Gale 2008).

Here we touch on the expression of personality or *terroir* as a distinct kind of value in wine, akin to the originality we value in artworks and other kinds of artefacts, and appreciated partly, again, for the skill involved in rendering inanimate objects expressive. Moreover, we can see how these qualities connect again to the fundamental value of "being interesting" and "rewarding attention" in virtue of being expressive of variety and difference. Although we seek out the familiar, we have an equally strong instinct against homogeneity and boredom: the more *terroirs* there are, and the more wines there are to express them, the better.

The problem of disagreement

Thus far I have sketched a rather general picture of how our perception of wine and the judgements we make about it may be informed by knowledge of a range of categorial information that is central to understanding the nature of wine, knowing how to appreciate it, and hence grounding the objectivity of our judgements about it. But I have been using the term "judgement" relatively loosely to cover a whole gamut of different types of assessment we make of wine, descriptive and evaluative alike, and the account I've sketched may seem perfectly suited to accommodating a realist position about the nature of the properties of wine. In fact, however, there are certain problems for the realist lurking in the ways that categorial information moulds our evaluative judgements of wine.

As we saw in Chapter 2, certain evaluative judgements employ what philosophers refer to as "thick" terms or concepts. That is, they will be applied to objects partly in virtue of descriptive, non-evaluative criteria. An example of such a term, outside the confines of wine talk, is "garish", which partly involves a negative evaluation but can only legitimately be applied to objects that have many bright, clashing colours. These are properties that are apparently straightforwardly perceptual, descriptive and hence objective. Thus we may be able, through the type of metaphorical conventions we have already discussed, to give an entirely satisfactory account of the meanings of and truth-conditions for certain evaluative terms applied to wine, as we saw in the case of "pretentious".

Now, such evaluations are no problem for the realist account of wine judgement if the evaluative part of these terms consists in there being a real negative value in the wine to which the responses of experts correspond, at least when they get things right. But is it really plausible to think of values in this way?

One reason to think not is that, even when we are concerned with the application of thick terms to objects, there is often still a question about deciding whether the descriptive conditions are sufficiently in place to warrant the evaluation. How brightly coloured and clashing do colours have to be for an object to be, *really*, garish? A similar question can be asked about "balanced". Now balance, as we have seen, is a very thick term indeed, and we can easily give a pretty straightforward account of the real properties of wine necessary for it to be balanced *in general terms*. But when it comes to discerning whether a particular wine is balanced, things become more complicated and individual tasters may differ in their assessments.

Given that subjective evaluations are involved, and that there may be more than one point at which a wine is balanced, why think, as the realist must, that in cases of disagreement there will always be only one right answer? Recall Smith's realist account of disagreement, which he claims will always be explained either (a) in terms of personal preference, or (b) by reference to different particular thresholds and sensitivities in certain individuals or populations. I think both of these factors actually undermine the realist's claim and point rather towards a certain relativist picture of taste.

We can begin to see this by turning to the ill-tempered and unusually stark debate between the famous wine experts Jancis Robinson and Robert Parker concerning the overall quality of the 2003 Château Pavie. Robinson assessed it thus: "Completely unappetising overripe aromas. Why? Porty sweet. Port is best from the Douro not St. Emilion. Ridiculous wine more reminiscent of a late-harvest Zinfandel than a red Bordeaux with its unappetising green notes". Parker, in contrast, thought it a great wine and commented that it "does not taste at all (for my palate) as described by Jancis".[1]

Smith says of this debate that the disparity between their verdicts:

---

1. Discussions of this dispute can be found in various places. For a good summary see www.jancisrobinson.com/articles/winenews0422 and www.decanter. com/news/48406.html (both accessed September 2010).

tended to obscure the level of agreement there was between them about the actual characteristics of the wine. The *very same qualities* in the wine, identified by Parker and singled out for praise as signs of the pleasure to be afforded by drinking this wine in the future, were criticized by Robinson as symptoms of excess and a lack of respect for Bordeaux-style wine making.

(2007b: n.26, emphasis added)

The question I wish to pursue is whether this assessment is right; that the very same qualities are identified by each. Part of the difficulty of this case is, as Smith says, that the dispute is largely based on personal preferences for different styles, and where personal preference is the primary issue we have clear disagreement, but nothing that affects realism. At the heart of Robinson's criticism was the perception that the Château Pavie was not a "Bordeaux-style" wine, and more specifically, that *as* a St Emilion it was an "aberration". Judged relative to these (correct) categories, in light of her expectations relative to them, and her own personal preferences for certain styles of wine, Robinson's remarks are perfectly understandable. Judged as a "Zinfandel", for example, her assessment may have been far more favourable and the "overripeness" and "sweetness" appreciated.

On the other hand, Parker's personal preferences for big, fruity, "overripe", intense and alcoholic wines are well documented and account for his favourable evaluation, even judged against the "Bordeaux" category. One way of understanding his judgement is that his personal preferences overrode any categorial qualms he may have harboured. Alternatively, Parker might be less sensitive to, or interested in, certain stylistic variations and category constraints than Robinson.[2]

In any case, we could, as Smith suggests, try to see it as just a difference in personal preferences directed at the very same objective properties of the wine that both disputants perceive equally clearly. If these preferences are both equally justified relative to equally justified categorial perceptions, this will be a greater problem for the realist than Smith acknowledges, because the wine will be legitimately ascribed incompatible values: there will be no one right answer about which values it possesses. But I think an even graver problem arises if we interpret the dispute as not merely about personal preference but about how the perceptible properties of the wine are *perceived* relative to background category judgements and preferences.

That is, there is a very important sense in which Parker and Robinson are tasting different things, perceiving the taste and smell properties in different ways, relative to different expectations and values.[3] She perceived the fruit aromas as "overripe", whereas he did not. Is there a fact of the matter about whether the aromas

---

2. Interestingly, in light of the comments on the intrinsic values of wine *qua* wine I aired above, one could perhaps indict Parker for (at least implicitly) supporting the homogenization of wine styles, thereby undermining variety, and the traditional "stylistic" values of individuality and the expression of *terroir*. This would be a serious and potentially damaging failure of taste.

3. Cf. Bender (2001) for a different account.

are overripe, as the realist must claim? Or is it more plausible to think that both judgements may be equally well justified – and hence "objective" – relative to the different categories and preferences against which the wine is tasted?

It follows from the account of wine judgements I have been presenting that our perception of wine is influenced in part by those factors that make up the expert's compendium of knowledge. Some such perception is relatively impermeable; namely, that involving basic taste and smell perceptions and the descriptive judgements these ground. Both Robinson and Parker detect the fruit aromas, and perhaps even agree on the type of fruit detected. But as soon as we enter the territory of evaluation, and evaluative metaphors, the *ways in which* even these base properties are perceived will depend heavily on interpretation, judgement, expectation, values and preferences that may vary even between experts. What counts as being "overripe"? It seems to be thoroughly a matter of evaluative difference, where the blameless disagreement is not just explicable in terms of personal preference.

Now quite often there will be a great deal of agreement here and enough in play to ground one right answer. But there is not enough, I contend, to support the realist's thesis that disagreements will always be resolvable in principle because, as in the case above, there will be occasions where, arguably, critics are *not* tasting the very same thing in the same way, in which case the judgements will be incommensurable, and both may be right. This, I think, is reason to be a non-realist about taste, at least for those evaluative judgements that affect the way in which the perceptible properties of the wine taste to the perceiver. But let's not be detained by this subtle philosophical dispute, for there are more important issues at stake than the labels we attach to our positions.

If we still wish to choose a winner in such disputes, we shall have to take a different turn in the argument and try to decide whose categories and background preferences are the right ones. I contended earlier that there are correct categories in which to judge wines, but the truth in this masks some complex issues, for in certain cases wines may be perceived and judged relative to incompatible, but equally legitimate, categories. This is an inevitable implication of the fact that categories encompass both the very broad and the very narrow. Walton himself gives a nice example of this, stating that individual Giacommetti sculptures can be seen as ethereal and emaciated relative to the category "sculpture", but relative to the narrower category "Giacommeti sculptures", they may become full of wiry strength and vitality. As there is no question of deciding which category is *the* right one, in such a case neither class of judgements can be deemed wrong.

There is an interesting phenomenon at work here. As in the case of regarding artworks, one may, as it were, switch between different experiences and judgements of wine. For example, it seems that I could – within certain perceptual limits – choose to taste a red wine as a New World or Old World, a South African Pinot Noir or a French Burgundy, and my various assessments of the wine will change accordingly.

So, we could hold that Parker was judging the Pavie not against the traditional Bordeaux category – and understandably, because it has contra-standard features for that category, as Robinson noted – but against a new, more flexible "Bordeaux" category, involving attributes that were standard for this new style of Bordeaux. In short, we could hold that Parker was invoking a new category, with the result being that the same wine will be given incompatible attributes. If so, then we would need to assess the validity of this category, whether it had developed stable norms and conventions of appreciation, what the intention of the winemaker was, and whether the values it put forward for appreciation were worth upholding or not. It might turn out, in light of this, that Parker's "category" will be rejected as illegitimate, but it might not; it might just be seen as a different way of tasting the wines of Bordeaux.[4]

We might, then, find ourselves with competing reasons for evaluation. On the one hand, the current categories of appreciation for Bordeaux wines allow certain styles and values to flourish, but, on the other hand, we ought to take into account the intentions of winemakers aiming for a certain Parker style and achieving it. Deciding between different values can become a fool's game, and the fluidity of categories and flux of wine styles pose real problems for the realist account. Indeed, as I shall note

---

4. Cf. the recent similar conflicting judgements of Parker and Robinson about the 2009 Cos d'Estournel.

below, they also pose problems for any account willing to defend objectivity.

Yet more threatening to the realist account is the existence of significant differences in perceptual discriminatory capacities between different populations of tasters. We noted earlier that some research seems to suggest that the perception of certain properties, such as sweetness in wine, may be culturally relative. Perhaps this amounts to a difference in perceptual sensitivity, and in Chapter 1 we saw evidence to suggest that some people are supertasters for at least some chemical properties. But if this is the case it is not at all clear that disputes based on actual differences in sensitivity will be resolvable, for in that case tastes really will be subjective; we will literally be tasting different things. Moreover, there is here simply no question of which one is superior or right; that is, there is no way of deciding which sensitivity-group should set the correct standard (see Bender 2008 for discussion).

In sum, it is doubtful for these reasons whether realism provides us with the right account of wine tasting practice and objectivity or can plausibly account for the nature of disagreement. But what exactly is the alternative? I have been defending throughout this book the idea that wine tasting is not subjective, for there are standards, conventions and expertise that ensure the objectivity of the practice and the judgements made on the basis of it. Yet, given the problems we have just seen in respect of the objectivity of evaluative judgements, how can we accommodate disagreement and yet maintain the objective stance?

Defending relativism

All is not lost. The problems we have raised pose serious threats to a realist account of objectivity, but it does not follow that we must abandon objectivity altogether. We can start by reminding ourselves that given the subtlety and fallibility of our taste and smell perception, the difficulty of translating our experiences into words, and the vast amount of information required for genuine expertise, many disagreements will be explicable in terms of certain failings in these respects. Where, as in the case of the Robinson–Parker dispute, different norms and standards seem to render the disagreement more deeply entrenched, there is frequently still room for reasoning and argument to play a role in the decision-making process, along some of the lines I indicated as being involved in choosing between categories. In such cases, disagreements may well prove resolvable. A similar observation is well made by John Bender:

> With the help of appropriate real-life wine comparisons, mightn't I be able to bring you around to see that those classically styled Cahors just have more to offer, and that your standard for a good Cahors needs to be appropriately revised? I can see a dispute, say, between two tasters, being resolved by a rethinking of their standards ("maybe zin-fandels *can* carry that huge amount of alcohol with some level of grace"), or a realization on the part of one that they have overstated the case in the particular instance

("well, come to think of it, this wine really doesn't lack fruit, does it?")... Perhaps the refinement of standards can be conceived as objective; through argument and a resulting greater acuity, one can become a better taster and make more subtle but also more exact judgements.

(2008: 131)

The objectivity of our judgements will always be grounded in part on the perceptible properties we can point to as providing reasons for judging the wine as we do, for using that metaphor and evaluation rather than another, and on the amenability of our evaluations to the process of reasoning. This is where Hume's theory and the analogy with colours falls short, for colour perception does not depend in part on evaluative differences nor on reasoning. As I noted earlier, if the only relations between the wine and us were brute causal ones, we would not get very far in expressing our complex experiences and accessing the values of which wine is capable. And, clearly, the establishment of the categories I outlined, and the norms they ground relative to expertise are indeed *normative*, in the sense that they imply certain standards of appreciation. They give us guidelines as to what to look for in order to *understand* and properly appreciate wine.

Where do these norms come from? From values inherent in the wine and the experiences to which they can give rise, experiences that in part depend on, but are not limited solely to, mere physical thresholds, for they can be partially shaped and moulded by those cognitive and evaluative factors we have noted.

How, again, can we account for disagreement here? How are we to know whether to revise our own standards, or those of our opponent? And how should we go about revising standards? Partly, I suggest, we decide whether those other standards involve a better *understanding* of the wine and whether we can *see the point* of them. They can, if appropriate, be justified by reasons and explanations that render the evaluations appropriate (see also Sweeney 2008).

Clearly levels of agreement may differ along various axes here, concerning for example: how specific the judgements are – "this is a particularly subtle expression of the Mourvèdre grape"; whether they are overall evaluations of quality – "this is a fantastic, beautiful wine"; evaluations involving comparisons – "this Syrah is a bit more refined than that one"; and the role of personal preferences in taste and vocabulary. What you call emaciated I might call merely slender; what you call coarse I call refreshingly aggressive; what you call extrovert and charming I call show-off and arrogant; what you label as cashmere texture I call silk texture. One need not expect wine experts to agree precisely on each and every metaphorical evaluation or description, any more than one would expect art or music critics to.

But such disagreement does not by itself preclude reasoned discussion about our respective judgements, and the ability to "see the point" of the respective ascriptions. There is a continuum on which emaciated and slender, coarse and aggressive, arrogant and extroverted, cashmere and silk lie in close enough relation to each other for judgements to make sense and for disagreements to be explained. If you call the tannins of a wine aggressive, whereas I

call them refined, then that may mark a possibly irresolvable difference in taste. Alternatively, however, it may be explained with
reference to a range of normative factors that can account for
such marked disagreement: I have a cold; I've not compared it to
other relevantly similar wines; I am inexperienced with limited
background knowledge; I have failed to master the conventional
vocabulary, and so on.

Partly, however, what is involved in reasoning and seeing
the point will sometimes involve ineliminably evaluative issues,
namely, whether the wine is more *rewarding* tasted in some new
light, or whether that way of categorizing its qualities undermines
some important value or other. This is what makes it difficult, and
sometimes impossible, to choose in cases where the dispute is a
deeply entrenched one involving the choice between fundamental
but fluid categories and fundamental wine values, as was evinced
in the case of Château Pavie 2003 and can be witnessed in recent
clashes over the merits of the 2009 vintage of Right Bank Bordeaux. Some experts have lauded these wines for their expressive
power and enormous, concentrated flavours, while others have
derided them as clichéd and sacrificing the traditional virtues of
their appellations and *terroirs*. It is not at all obvious to me that
there is a right view here, because at stake are essentially incommensurable values; although there may be room for argument
about the long-term threat to the existence of certain styles and
values.

In sum, I think we are left with the following philosophical
position on the objectivity of wine judgements. The picture is

what we might call a *defeasible* account of the justification of aesthetic judgements. To be able to justify an aesthetic ascription we must be able to explain why the non-evaluative features justify the attribution of *F* rather than *G*, where this allows that there be possible defeating considerations that would undermine the judgement but which do not in fact obtain. At the very least, in the face of marked evaluative disagreements, one must be able to recognize the reasons given as justifying (or not) the appropriateness of the opponent's view. One must be able to "see the point" of the judgement, even where this may involve, in cases of extreme disagreement, an explanation appealing to (perhaps irreconcilable) differences in "taste". For these reasons the mark of objectivity in wine judgement is perhaps best thought of in terms such as appropriateness rather than truth.

Understanding differences is not, however, the same thing as reconciling them. There is no guarantee that for some disputes, particularly certain evaluative ones, there will not be more than one correct or appropriate way of describing or evaluating the wine, and these may be incompatible relative to different norms and standards in the ways mentioned, where there is no absolutely right way of deciding among competing norms and categories, for these themselves will be *evaluative choices*.

For those descriptive judgements grounded in one-to-one correlations of chemical properties with physiological responses in us, and for metaphorical judgements that involve established conventions governing their use (or that can be cashed out in terms of descriptive properties and judgements), we can expect widespread agreement and uphold the objectivity of our judgements. Given the existence of supertasters and certain cultural differences in perceptual thresholds and discrimination, we should expect agreement and convergence within those groups too.

What we now have is not a realist position, but nor is it a sceptical one. Instead it is what I will call a limited relativist position: limited because, *as a matter of fact*, many categories and norms are clearly established as correct, and the judgements of wine made relative to them will be truth-apt. When it comes to some of the many different types of evaluative judgements we make about wine, however, I think we will find that there may sometimes be more than one incompatible but equally well-justified – and hence "objective" – judgement that can be applied to it. How we decide between competing experts in these cases will itself be partly an evaluative matter, and there are many, perhaps incommensurable, values that may be relevant to this choice.

Matters are thus inevitably complicated when it comes to weighing up and ranking the various values that wine can possess. Some connoisseurs might prefer rusticity to urbanity in their wines, value boldness and brashness over elegance and refinement, and prefer their tannins to be on the large and firm side. Some will prefer the charms of Burgundy to the Rhône, or the up-front fruitiness of Australian Rieslings to the subtler kerosene notes of the whites of Alsace. Some may prefer the typical tastes and textures of one *terroir* or one varietal over another. But this is no more problematic for determining the values intrinsic to wine than it is for defending the objectivity of our judgements concerning them; subjective taste and value, remember, can come apart. Just as there is room in the world for Schoenberg and Schubert, Hodgkin and Pissarro, Chesterton and Proust, so is there room for a proliferation of values and stylistic "tastes" to flourish.

We must recognize, however, that by making such allowances, what counts as being balanced, for example, may well differ from style to style. There will always be certain physical limitations on the absolute threshold proportions of the different elements of wine – sugar, tannins, acid, alcohol – that secure a minimum degree of balance for wine in general, but the precise proportions may allow various degrees and dimensions of difference depending on style and preference. The sharp, piercing acidity of Chablis, or the low alcohol of Moselle Rieslings may appear to make such wines unbalanced to palates untutored in them, but represent the values characteristic of those wine styles, and of specific varietals, to their appreciators who will perceive their elements to be in balance *relative to* those styles.

Have we now suddenly lost hold of the normative force of our judgements, of the notion of understanding? I don't think so, for we have not lost hold of the various structures and categories governing appreciation. We should not think that what counts as elegant in one of Schoenberg's dodecaphonic compositions would be recognizable as elegant were it, bizarrely, to crop up in a Brahms sextet, but this does not entail that we cannot make sense of the description-evaluation "elegant" applied to both, relative to the different categories against which their compositions should be assessed. This observation touches on some deep and complex issues concerning the nature of aesthetic and artistic value, and it is high time, therefore, that we turned to an exploration of these.

5

The Aesthetic Value of Wine
Beauty, Art, Meaning and Expression

The domain of the aesthetic

Many of the purported hallmarks of tastes and smells that, as we saw in Chapter 1, are used to question their metaphysical and epistemological status, have also been called on to challenge their capacity – and hence, by extension, the objects they constitute, such as wine – to be of aesthetic interest and value. On the rare occasions that philosophers in the past deigned to discuss tastes and smells in relation to aesthetic interest and value, they generally did so either to exclude them from the domain of the aesthetic altogether, invoking a putative distinction between genuine aesthetic value and merely sensuous pleasure; or to claim that whatever aesthetic value is possessed by tastes and smells is trivial, attenuated or otherwise lacking in significance.

Despite his otherwise robust defence of the importance and value of wine in the life of rational beings, Roger Scruton's voice has been the loudest and most cogent here, but increasingly also the loneliest. For most contemporary philosophers writing on wine seem loath to dismiss its aesthetic value, although they remain ambivalent about the precise character and degree of such value that wine can possess. In part, I think, this is because the discussion of aesthetic value is often intertwined with the closely related, but by no means identical, question of whether wine can be art. Even where the two issues are explicitly distinguished, the kinds of aesthetic values attributed to wine are more often than not conceived in terms of, compared to, and contrasted with the particular aesthetic values that artworks can manifest.

Unsurprisingly in this light, wine, more often than not, comes off looking second best, offering trivial rather than serious pleasure, and lacking the intimations of intellectual contemplation and cognitive rewards associated with *understanding, meaning, interpretation* and *expression*, which many have seen as essential to the aesthetic value of artworks.

In order to consider these claims carefully, it might appear obvious that we need to commence with a conception of aesthetic value, interest and experience. Yet this is a treacherous place of embarkation, for the history of philosophical aesthetics is awash with thwarted and vain attempts to capture in a philosophical definition the nature of the "aesthetic", differentiated in part by whether they put an emphasis on a particular experience, attitude or set of objects and their properties as the relevant source of aesthetic value. But it is not an entirely fruitless enterprise, for such attempts have in common an appeal to the idea – to be traced ultimately to Immanuel Kant's great work the *Critique of Judgement* –

that an aesthetic experience essentially involves appreciating some object "for its own sake" and, concomitantly, that the notions of aesthetic judgement and aesthetic value can be explicated partly in these terms.[1]

Scruton takes his account of aesthetic interest from the same tradition and, drawing on many of the kinds of features of tastes and smells examined in Chapter 1, he argues that the aesthetic experiences of sight and hearing essentially involve "thought" about the object at which they are directed. In contrast, he says, our purely sensory, gustatory pleasures lack "the intellectual intimations that are the hallmark of aesthetic interest. Sensory pleasure is available whatever the state of your education; aesthetic pleasure depends upon knowledge, comparison and culture" (2007: 3).

Well, we have by now gathered sufficient evidence to demonstrate that, by these criteria, wine possesses (*contra* Scruton) all of the features essential to being an object of aesthetic appreciation. Our experiences of the tastes and smells constituting wine can involve high levels of discriminatory ability, large stores of knowledge and expertise, and sophisticated imaginative capacities employed in categorizing the objects of experience and deploying judgements about them. Indeed, I have suggested that they must do so if they are to constitute a proper *understanding* and appreciation of wine. Our judgements of wine are riddled with the kinds

---

1. One of the clearest attempts to sketch an account along these lines is that of Malcolm Budd (1995; 2002: 14).

of reasoning and normativity that are central dimensions of aesthetic experience and judgement.

It is important here to disentangle the domain of aesthetic value from that of artistic value. For the former extends well beyond the realm of art, encompassing arguably anything on which we can fix our attention – and perhaps even abstract thoughts, such as those characteristic of mathematics and philosophy – and paradigmatically including non-artefacts, such as the objects of nature, which provide us with some of our deepest and most thrilling aesthetic experiences.

As applied to artworks, the conception of aesthetic interest on which Scruton's scepticism is built can seem unwarrantedly narrow, overly intellectual and demanding. After all, there appear to be artworks that do not, and are not intended to, reward cognitively sophisticated thought; many abstract, non-representational pictures seem to be good examples of this, or where they do, like Rothko's pictures, seek to arouse and express abstract thought it's at least not clear why tastes and smells cannot be similarly evocative. Or consider the kinds of decorative patterns one sees recur throughout Islamic art and architecture, and the vast amount of instrumental music that also fails to fit the intellectual bill. We would not want to deny the tag "aesthetic" to these kinds of works of art. However, we might be inclined to think the aesthetic rewards of which such works are capable to be limited.

This is really the key point. There remains the possibility that in the hierarchy of aesthetic value wine *in general* is of little significance when compared with other objects of aesthetic interest, as the patterned meanderings of a Morris design might compare with a Caravaggio. Perhaps wine has less aesthetic potential, precluded by the nature of tastes and smells from manifesting the various values and virtues we associate with the cultivation of more important areas of our aesthetic lives. Indeed, this has been a common theme even among philosophers who have otherwise devoted considerable time to defending the aesthetic value of tastes and smells and the aesthetic interest of wine. Here, for instance, are some of the relatively disparaging remarks made by Frank Sibley:

> For aesthetic importance there is presumably no case for setting a Château Lafite against the *Missa Solemnis*, or even perhaps against a reasonably good sonnet.   (2001: 249)

> Even if tastes and smells are possible objects of aesthetic interest and delight, their importance is no doubt minor, even, some might think, *necessarily* trifling; and probably even someone who saw them as simple paradigms would be prepared to allow that, in aesthetic value, the finest perfume or wine is not to be compared with that of the greatest art.   (212, emphasis added)

> Perfumes and flavours, natural or artificial, are necessarily limited: unlike the major arts, they have no expressive connections with emotions, love or hate, grief, joy, terror, suffering, yearning, pity, or sorrow – or with plot or character development.   (249)

More recently, Tim Crane has claimed that although wine can contain messages, and can be representational in the wide sense of conveying information about things external to it, it "has no intellectual or cognitive content" (2007: 147), and many have echoed the position of John Bender in declaiming: "I do not believe a wine can be sad, but I do think it can be poised or flashy" (2008: 129).

If these thoughts are on the right track then perhaps there are also practical, even moral, implications to be drawn from them. Given the myriad encroachments on our time, and the serious value that is claimed for artworks, perhaps life is just too short (and money too valuable) to bother cultivating a taste for fine wine. Is it an essentially frivolous pastime? Is it impossible for wine to be *about* things, to possess cognitive content, to offer perspectives on the world? Is it impossible for wine to be expressive of emotional states? Why can't wines be sad if they can be poised and flashy? These are perhaps the most interesting and difficult questions that can be asked about the nature and appreciation of wine.

Drinking wine as art

Some of the concerns about the aesthetic value of wine form part of an explanation as to why it has been frequently excluded from the status of art. Such an explanation, note, would appear to hinge on an evaluative classification of art, whereby only artefacts with a sufficient amount of the right kind of value achieve art status.

Thus one might set out to create an artwork and fail, in virtue of one's incompetence, to create art at all. Such evaluative classifications of art are not very helpful, however, for we want to be able to label some things "bad art", to differentiate between good and bad art, and give reasons for the distinction. It is important to know what makes some art good, and how to avoid making some art bad.

The explanation also appeals implicitly to an equation between aesthetic and artistic value, but this too might be questioned. Arguably, not all of the values that art objects possess *qua* art – that is, the essentially artistic values they possess in virtue of being art – need be aesthetic. Many philosophers are pluralists about artistic value, insisting that art can have, for example, certain moral and cognitive values that are not aesthetic, but are nevertheless an essential part of a work's artistic value. Depending on what position one adopts in the contested territory concerning the relation between aesthetic and artistic value, the supposed inability of wine to manifest such values might count against its claims to artistic status *tout court* or allow it to achieve only relatively minor artistic value.

But what is the "concept of art"? Philosophical attempts to define art have fared little better than attempts to define the aesthetic, and the disputed nature of the category has been evident in popular, and not just intellectual, discussion ever since Marcel Duchamp boldly exhibited a urinal. One of the most long-standing philosophical definitions of art – the "institutional theory" – defines art as anything put forward for appreciation *as* art by members of the institution the "art world". Pretty vacuous as a definition of art, you'd be right to think, but it does capture the large kernel of truth that art status in our contemporary world does seem relatively easy to acquire, often requiring merely that someone with sufficient clout in the art world – a Charles Saatchi, for example – takes a liking to something or somebody and chooses to purchase and exhibit the pieces to others who have similar tastes and interests.

Such a "definition" simply reflects the fact that the concept of art is extremely malleable: liable to be stretched and distorted according to indefinable and elusive whims and fashions that frequently have less to do with the objects' intrinsic values, and more to do with multifarious political, personal and economic interests. Indeed, one of the most striking features of the phenomenon of contemporary art is the subsuming of standards of evaluation beneath the dominant subjective preferences of the arbiters of taste who are so influential in the art world, and the concomitant divorce effected between such preferences and the actual values of the objects that are put forward for appreciation.

Given the flexible and loosely anchored nature of "art", why haven't its boundaries been extended to include, for instance, food and drink? After all, purportedly frivolous claims that a great wine can be an artwork are just as often mirrored by claims that great food dishes can be works of art, and that great chefs are artists. Indeed, as haute cuisine, along with fine wine, has begun to seep more and more deeply into popular consciousness, this has become something of a serious debate.

There are, however, a number of other factors frequently cited against including wine under the umbrella of "art". Wine is consumed simultaneously with its appreciation; the object itself is destroyed, leaving no trace in the world once drunk. But we do not generally countenance works of art going out of existence like this as being an essential part of their appreciation; indeed, we generally hold the contrary position. Of course, one might think that the wine itself is not thereby consumed if we identify the wine object not with the particular tokens existing in the particular bottles that are drunk, but, say, with the vintage as a whole. Wine may be analogous to music in this respect, in that we must differentiate the music existing as a composition from the individual performances of it that are given.

There is something to this analogy, but of course as Crane (2007) points out, the token bottles of Château Margaux 2000 are actual *parts of* the type, physically constituting it, in a way that is fundamentally different from the abstract relation that musical performances have to the musical composition. As he says, the "wine object" itself is scattered throughout the world, existing only in its instances. Moreover, that vintage will cease to exist when the last bottle is drunk, but musical compositions will not thus cease to be, even if they never happen to be performed again. Finally, vintages themselves are transient, ephemeral objects that change over time, to the extent that it becomes debateable whether any two bottles of the same vintage even contain identical stuff.

Yet these by themselves do not seem to be particularly powerful objections to wine's aspiration to art status. After all, some contemporary works of art are similarly transient – recall the delicate environmental art of Andy Goldsworthy – nor does there seem to be anything essential to the concept of art that excludes such ephemerality.

These considerations suggest that the question of whether wine is or can be art might be unanswerable, or that there simply is no fact of the matter, and hence that the question itself is rather hollow, given the unlikelihood of ever agreeing non-arbitrarily on the necessary and sufficient conditions for something to be art. Or perhaps we should conclude, more charitably, that it is not so much a philosophical issue, as a sociocultural and/or psychological one.

In large part, I think, this is absolutely right: from a philosophical point of view there are few questions as uninspiring as the question "What is art?" However, given the significant place that art has in our culture, there is something important in trying to understand whether something is art, in so far as labelling something as art – however subject to idiosyncratic whims and fashions the label might be – generally compels us to look at what might be a very familiar or unremarkable object in an entirely new light. The unmade bed is no longer *just* a bed; its particular qualities are now presented for our attention, and perhaps they will also reward it. In virtue of being placed for appreciation in a gallery the object has now been imbued with some kind of meaning and given a status from which we expect (at times wrongly, as Duchamp pointed out) certain rewards – experiential and intellectual – to follow. We stop before it, contemplate it, try to understand the point of it, and the intention of the artist and gallery in exhibiting it.

In short, we regard an object differently when invited to regard it *as* an art object. Although the unmade bed in the gallery may be perceptually indistinguishable from the unmade bed at home, we perceive them very differently, and in a way that by now should be familiar to you. In the case of art objects our perception is imbued with those background thoughts involved in categorizing objects that we explored in the last chapter, where the category of art now provides a general framework for appreciation and affects the way in which we perceive the object.

The important point is this. Whether we choose to encompass wine (or food, or gardens, bullfighting or football) under the concept of "art" or not, and to designate winemakers or chefs "artists", when we are aware of the values that wine can possess, and when we know that we are confronted by a "fine wine", we attend to it carefully, with thought, and we attempt to *understand* it in the expectation of getting some kind of evaluative reward for our efforts. This understanding makes sense in virtue of the fact that wine is an artefact, a product of human aims and designs. In short, wine is the result of intention and this is crucial to grasping the aesthetic value and significance with which it can be imbued. In these respects there is some point to attempts to elevate fine wine on to the pedestal of art or to, as it were, drink it as art. Anyone who denies that there is anything to understand in appreciating fine wine does not comprehend the cognitive role played in our appreciation of it, fails to see the ways in which tastes and smells can be *intentionally structured* to reward such appreciation, and will be unable to explain the normative force of our judgements concerning it. These aspects differentiate the nature of such appreciation from, for instance, the merely sensuous pleasure one gets from having a hot bath.

For these reasons, one *ought* to try to notice the delicate balance of the La Conseillante, one *should* make some effort to see in what respects it is *better as a wine* than the generic red Côtes de Bourg, and if one does not perceive these things one will have missed something of value that is there to be experienced. This notion of understanding is partly applied to the object of appreciation, and partly to the intrinsic value of the experience itself. We talk about the qualities of the wine that are there to be appreciated, but our judgements about its values also involve communicating and sharing our experiences of these properties. Thus, in part what one understands when one takes the effort to appreciate a fine wine is the experience that such a wine can provide. There is a notion of "aesthetic understanding" here that is analogous to that at play in the appreciation of art when perceiving art objects as having the values they do (see Budd 1995). It is an essentially experiential notion: the thinking is, as it were, in the drinking.

In this light, we are now in a position to return finally to the question posed at the end of Chapter 2 and which has often been asked of the metaphysical status of artworks: what exactly is the object of appreciation when we critically taste and assess a wine? Is it an ordinary, everyday, physical object consisting of perceptible chemical compounds in the external world, as common sense suggests, or is it rather an imaginative, interpretive, experiential object that somehow arises out of physical reality? I think it is a combination of both, for if we are tasting appropriately, with knowledge and understanding, in all the ways we have discussed, the "experiential object" is not a hazy cloud of random associations, but is intrinsically connected to the physical reality that, after all, ultimately justifies the judgements we make of our experiences *of* the wine itself (see Sweeney 2008 for a good discussion of this).

Values of wine and values of art

Whatever its eventual shortcomings, the analogy with art is also useful for thinking of some of the values that wine can possess, albeit a potentially threatening one to the defender of the overall aesthetic interest of wine, *vis-à-vis* art.

The hierarchy of evaluative categories under which wines are subsumed, I noted in Chapter 4, is founded on the types of intrinsic value that wine can possess and manifest *qua* wine, and the best wines will manifest those values to the highest degree. Note that this general criterion of evaluation applies equally to other realms of appreciation. Test cricket, for instance, arguably represents that form of the game in which all the highest values – many of which are aesthetic – of which cricket *qua* cricket is capable are manifested. This remains true even where there are other forms of cricket that have their own virtues, values and vices, and forms of appreciation particular to them. Similarly, in each artistic genre there will be works that are great for the same sorts of reasons, where these reasons are operative in that particular genre.

But what are these intrinsic values of wine? In Chapter 4 I listed complexity, intensity, balance, personality and *terroir*, and I sketched some speculative reasons as to why such qualities might be intrinsically valued, to do with the nature of interest and attention, variety, surprise, the exercise of discriminatory abilities, and the discovery of pattern and unity amid variety.[2] It is noteworthy that, with the exception of *terroir*, these are all also generally accounted as central virtues in artworks. Obviously they will be manifested in different ways in wine, but one can all too easily stress the differences at the expense of the more striking parallels.

Some philosophers have in this light remarked on the various ways in which wine is like music. Wine tasters talk of the various aroma "notes" in wine, of harmony and dissonance, of expectation and revelation, of discerning patterns, and of change and development over time; and these are thought of, and appreciated partly, as intentionally structured. Perhaps it is not absurd to say that I am drowning in the ethereal sound of Tallis's *Spem in Alium* in something like the same sort of way that I am drowning in the ethereal taste and smell depths of the Château Haut-Brion, or that the floral notes of a Condrieu are in some way like the floral notes in a Debussy prelude. Moreover, like music, wines are also

---

2. There is an interesting question as to whether some of these values are properly aesthetic in nature, or rather cognitive, but we can steer clear of this issue for present purposes.

talked of in expressive terms, as displaying character and personality. Perhaps the expression of *terroir* can be thought of – or *drunk as* – a variation on a theme, where the theme is provided by the character of the varietal.

Or perhaps the analogy with architecture is closer. We talk of the volume and shape of wines, of their textures and contours, and we try to assess the interrelations among their structural features. It makes some sense to think of certain wines as gothic, and others perhaps as rococo. But of course wine is an essentially natural product while also being an artefact, so perhaps it is more like the pseudo-art of gardening in which the forces of nature are moulded by human design, and the constraints of natural growth in part determine the expressive and symbolic properties that we appreciate.

How far can we stretch these parallels without distorting the distinctive nature of wine and our appreciation of it? As I argued earlier, I suggest we can stretch them as far as is required to make sense of our experiences of wine and of our drinking it with understanding. How far is that? Not far enough, some philosophers will say, to endow wine with expression or meaning, and it is simply fanciful to claim otherwise, no matter how we actually do talk about wine. This fermented grape juice is simply not the kind of thing that can be genuinely expressive or meaningful, and the analogy with art, in so far as it's of any use at all, will stop at the level of a pseudo or minor art form. Perhaps winemaking is more akin to a craft. Whereas artworks can be truly expressive and imaginative, burrowing deeply into our moral and emotional lives, possessing meaning and cognitive content, providing insight into us and our world, the purveyors of craft use their skills mechanically in the service of a function that is external to the object itself. Art for art's sake, one might declaim, but wine for the sake of sensuous pleasure and intoxication.

Certainly this is not to denigrate the immense skills involved in fulfilling this function, in structuring tastes and smells in sophisticated ways, nor to deny the intrinsic values of balance, complexity and intensity integral to the nature of wine. But in the grand scheme of things, it might be thought, these values are of little relative importance and the aesthetic potential of wine very limited. In short, we have not yet slain the lurking suspicion that, in the world of absolute value, among the immense panoply of things we are able as human beings to contemplate and appreciate, wine must figure relatively lowly. It is this negative view of the aesthetic capacities of wine that we must now combat, by drawing on the notions of "representation", "expressive", and "expression", which are almost as loose, slippery, and unclear as those of "objectivity", "aesthetic" and "art", with which we have just been grappling.

Expressive wines

Paradigmatic expressive properties are those we attribute to sentient beings as *expressive of* psychological states. Perhaps the most obvious class of such states are emotions, but sentient beings can also, in various ways, express other states, including attitudes, ideas, values, worldviews, and so on. And the features of sentient beings that in part constitute expressive properties include a whole range of expressive behaviours: bodily movements, gestures and facial expressions; language; tone and pitch of voice, and so on.

We also attribute expressive properties to non-sentient, inanimate objects. The paradigmatic objects here are artworks. Certain works of art, such as representational paintings, films, or works of literary fiction, may be expressive partly by depicting or portraying people who are expressing certain psychological states. Such cases of expression-depiction might be held to be expressive in virtue of being parasitic on our ability to see human beings as expressive. There is much philosophical and psychological discussion about just how we experience the relevant features of human beings as expressive, and how we attribute expressive properties to them. Here is not the place to engage with these complex issues, and anyway, these are not the cases that interest me here. Rather, I am more concerned with cases like the ability of *a work itself* to be expressive. Van Gogh's pictures are expressive in this sense, even if they do not depict human subjects, and it is generally held that we can experience abstract instrumental music as expressive.

It is an interesting and difficult philosophical question just what such expressivity consists in. Nonetheless, it is normally taken for granted that music and painting are the kinds of things that can be genuinely expressive, even if this expressivity is ultimately, somehow, parasitic on the central case of human expression. Music, it is thought, really can express "sadness" – or something saliently similar – even if it is puzzling how this is possible. In contrast, although we can and do attribute expressive properties to non-art objects, it is often denied that such objects can be genuinely expressive even in the parasitic sense that music can be. So although wines are readily described as cheerful, attractive, sexy, sensually expressive, abrasive and authentic, philosophers have evinced scepticism about the appropriateness of such metaphors, but no such scepticism about the genuine applicability of expressive characteristics to artworks like abstract music. Why the difference?

As good a place to start as any is with Carolyn Korsmeyer's eloquent and insightful defence of the capacity of food to be expressive and meaningful. Korsmeyer points out that food can represent things by being used to denote them. To take one of her examples, one might make pale green leaf-shapes that seem to be made out of something cool and bland, like avocado, but in fact consist of pureed horseradish: "we could say that these are leaf-representations that metaphorically exemplify coolness but possess furious hotness" (2008: 33). She also gives the example of croissants, which were invented in Vienna in 1683 to celebrate the defeat of the Ottoman siege of the city. The crescent shape of the bun refers to the crescent moon on the Turkish flags and the fact that one "*devours* the crescent reenacts the defeat of the invaders, and perhaps also represents Christianity conquering Islam" (*ibid.*).

In these kinds of ways, she holds, food can be used symbolically and can take on expressive properties, such as being witty, playful or ironic. Furthermore, Korsmeyer claims that food and meals can convey certain kinds of meaning in virtue of the specific contexts in which they are produced, presented and consumed; indeed, food is capable of even cognitively complex "propositional understanding". As evidence of this, she recounts a fairy tale in which a father rejects his daughter for claiming that she loves him only "as fresh meat loves salt". Subsequently, at a lavish banquet the father is served meat without salt and suddenly realizes what his daughter meant.

According to Korsmeyer, the father comes to understand – in a thoroughly experiential way akin to experiential aesthetic understanding in the context of art works – the "truth"; he comes to realise "viscerally" that she really loved him (39).

Nonetheless, Korsmeyer is cautious in restricting the expressive capabilities of food, for she holds that, unlike art, the aesthetic and cognitive significance of food depends heavily on features of the context, and on personal and cultural associations. She notes that the "aesthetic functions of food exceed the qualities of the food itself" (44), and that unlike music and other fine arts, foods "require extended context to achieve their denotative and expressive meanings, that the items to eat *by themselves* do not always manage to carry their ritual or traditional or cultural significance" (45).

These purported limitations lie at the heart of concerns about the expressive capabilities of wine. Here again is Scruton, who claims that tastes and smells, being immune to intrinsic ordering and transition, acquire meaning by "association rather than expression" and by "context rather than content", unlike sounds structured as music "which can bear within themselves all the meaning that human beings are able to communicate". They are, he says, "free-floating and unrelated, unable to generate expectation, tension, harmony, suspension or release", characteristics which of course are the keys to music's ability to express emotion (2007: 5).

Now clearly wine too can take on symbolic significance and meaning, as it has done for millennia in religious contexts, and in early Greek thought, where Plato extolled its virtues in facilitating the philosophical and spiritual reflections in which the true, the good, and the beautiful became united. But can wine, in virtue of its *intrinsic* properties, be expressive and meaningful? I want to claim that it can be, and this, above all, is what makes wine, more than any other food or beverage, so special.

There is no doubt that association plays some role in the attribution of certain qualities to wine, but fine wines have expressive properties that are not reducible to mere association, and are as much properties of content as they are of context. I should note, however, that I am not convinced there is always a sharp distinction between association and expressiveness; it seems rather a question of degree. In any case, these expressive properties are attributes of the content of wine, I think, in large part in virtue of the role that intention, and its detection *in* the wine, plays in their attribution and justification. The role and recognition of intention in wine can suffice to turn mere association into expression.

The importance of intention is not always acknowledged, but wine is, after all, an artefact, intentionally created to have many (but obviously not all) of the properties it does as the result of an ensemble of decisions that relate to a range of different considerations. Just like in art, part of what we appreciate in fine wines is the achievement the wine represents as a manifestation of the winemaker's skill. Often these intentions can be known via the wine label, or with a little research, but as in art they can often be guessed at and at least in part reconstructed by tasting the wine. Whether we have understood a wine will therefore in part depend on whether we have detected the aims or failed aims of the winemaker in the wine.

Now it is certainly true that mass-produced, highly manufactured wines may be utterly bereft of expressive potential, and perhaps even of identifiable aims. And in many cases the relevant aims may be quite broad, the intention being primarily to create a certain general style of wine, such as crisp and clean, fruity, austere, subtle or complex. But in fine wines, some of these aims will be distinctly expressive. One of the key values that the role of intention unlocks in fine wines, and akin to a central value we recognize in artworks, is the uniqueness and individuality of the product. Wines are valued for their expressiveness, for their personality, and (more controversially) for their embodiment of *terroir*. This should be no surprise because such a value makes a wine more interesting than wines that are mass-produced and lacking in such qualities.[3] A nice example of this is given in the following appraisal by Jasper Morris of Domaine de la Romanée-Conti's Le Montrachet 2000:

---

3. For discussion, see Grahm (2008); Kramer (2008).

The domaine makes a point of picking its Montrachet as late as possible, often well after all the other producers have completed their harvest. Co-owner Aubert de Villaine has noticed across the years that grapes in Le Montrachet retain their acidity even if left late on the vine. This late picking results in extraordinary opulence and an almost monolithic intensity that speak more of the producer than the vineyard. But after time in the glass, the incredible character of the vineyard starts to show …

(Beckett 2008: 347)

The expression of *terroir* and personality is thus in part the result of the intentional act of the winemaker, and it takes great skill to marry the environment to the particular grape varieties used, to create a unique whole from an array of different parts. To the extent that a winemaker's intentions are successfully realized they are identifiable *in* the wine, and the more complex, expressive, original, true to *terroir* the wine is, the greater the achievement it represents. This is so even where the winemaker's explicit intentions are to let the winemaking process be as natural as possible, for it is human guidance that selects and allows this process to succeed. As Paul Draper, the chief winemaker of Ridge Wines says:

not only did the wine with our guidance and care make itself, but you could find distinctive character in the wines that you hadn't created by blending or adding or subtracting, but that actually came from a piece of ground. So it struck me that if you were really talking about wine as a natural product, as something authentic, then you should be seeking out those parcels, those pieces of land, where there was individuality of character and real quality in the grapes themselves. You would tend the vineyard and guide the transformation in the cellar, but the wine would reflect nature and the natural process.

(Jefferson & Draper 2007: 201–2)

Partly connected with the expression of *terroir*, the most complex and sophisticated wines are held to express individuality and uniqueness, and they are often described as having personality or character, and being expressive of, among other things, certain human-like character traits. For example, wines can be joyful, refined, friendly, attractive. Wines that do not bow to the pressures of commercialization are described as authentic, or sincere, and wines that "try" and "fail" to be something that they are not can be pretentious, dishonest or commercial. In contrast, very complex wines that change a great deal, that do not settle, that defy easy analysis, might be called capricious or seductive.

Note that we do not readily describe food and dishes in these terms, nor indeed any other beverage, suggesting that it is not just arbitrary trains of random associations in virtue of which we appreciate and describe wines with the complexity we do, and hold them in such high esteem. It is in virtue of qualities intrinsic to the nature of wine and the experiences it provides us with that account for this. It is worth noting that Scruton himself allows that through the taste of *terroir* in the perception of fine wine, "where that means not merely the soil, but the customs and ceremonies that had sanctified it … we are knowing – by acquaintance, as it were – the history, geography and customs of a community" (2007: 16). He holds, however, that this knowledge and value come from association rather than expression, from context rather than content.

But I think the explanation works the other way around; we only recognize the associations because they arise from the content of the wine.

So, wines are made in certain ways, embodying certain decisions, and these can be detected as expressive properties in the wine itself. Furthermore, I suggest, very fine wines can possess expressive properties that are not merely internal to the nature of wine, so to speak, but concern more general "life values". This is difficult to spell out precisely, but I think that wines can be expressive of certain attitudes and views concerning, for example, civilized life, sophistication, simplicity, the rustic/rural versus the urbane/urban, elegance, authenticity, variety, subtlety, and so on. That is, calling a wine elegant or rustic may refer not just to the intrinsic properties of the wine that it exemplifies, but to an array of attitudes to life and the world that have allowed it to come to be made in just this way. Choosing between, for instance, Old World and New World wines, or between Burgundy and Bordeaux, will in turn reflect some of these values expressed in the wines chosen.

Far from being the mechanical products of craft, therefore, there is a deep truth reflected in the English word "husbandry" and the

French word *elevage*, which together capture the way in which a natural product is nurtured and gently educated and influenced and impressed with qualities in order to express certain values, some of which will include perspectives on the world and our appreciation of it.

So, wine can, as such, embody certain kinds of meaning in virtue of possessing expressive properties that – through the role of intention and the categorial considerations sketched – are genuinely part of the content of the wine and not just garnered through contingent associations and extraneous contextual considerations, even though these too may play a central role. Expressiveness, that is, cannot be simply reduced to either content or association, assuming one can even make sense of a rigid distinction between the two. As such, wine can be, in short, a genuine expressive vehicle.

It might be objected at this point that, in spite of my earlier contention that wine differs in its expressive capacities from other related objects of consumption, I have now unwittingly opened the floodgates to anything, in principal, becoming an expressive object. There no longer seems to be any obvious reason why we should impose limits on the types of objects that can be appreciated as expressive. There are, after all, food critics, expert chocolatiers, people who appreciate trains, whiskey, clouds, and no doubt a whole raft of other things that people can and do spend a great deal of effort in discriminating and evaluating. Is this a genuine worry? On the one hand, such activities do not strike me as inherently ludicrous or illegitimate. Nonetheless, on the other hand,

I think there are some sorts of limits on expressivity, and I shall merely gesture at two potential candidates here.

First, expressive potential has much to do with the role of, and recognition of, intention and skill, so while it is no doubt possible to provide an appreciative framework within which any number of different types of object (from piles of gravel to perfumes) can become expressive vehicles, I think a lack of direct human intention restricts the range and perhaps intensity of expressive properties. For example, "wild" nature – as opposed to, say, gardens, and perhaps certain types of cultural/agricultural landscapes – may be seen as expressive of certain moods and feelings (e.g. the "eeriness" of an empty moor; the "solitude" of the sea) but only within a relatively limited range. Second, I suggest that some objects simply possess certain properties, and complex arrangements of them that, in interaction with particular physical and/or cultural characteristics of human beings, provide more expressive potential than others, and which allow wine, for example, to be a more expressive object than, say, beer.

Inevitably, it is an extremely difficult matter to determine the truth of such claims, other than by simply pointing to current practices, and all I would stress here is that expressiveness involves such a heady combination of physical properties and their interaction with perceptual, psychological and cultural capacities and characteristics, institutions, norms, conventions, practices and so on, that the notion is, I think, far more opaque than philosophers have recognized. But this opacity fails to obscure the expressive properties that we readily attribute to wine in order to communicate some of the valuable experiences we receive from drinking it.

This brings us to the final issue. Even if we grant that wines can be expressive of certain values and perspectives in the ways I have listed, one might well insist that *expressiveness* falls short of *expression*, which latter concept refers paradigmatically to the expression of some emotional state. One might object that, even granted the expressive powers I have advocated for it, wine cannot, as music supposedly can, express human emotions such as sadness, joy or anger.

Emotional wines

At first glance it might seem crazy to claim that wine can express emotion, and that however liberal we are in the use of metaphors to ascribe human characteristics to this chemical compound of fermented grape juice, it simply does not make sense to describe a wine as sad or angry or hopeful. The contrast here is supposed to be with artistic expression, and in particular with the purported capacity of abstract art – especially instrumental music – to express emotion. The comparison with music is central because sounds, like tastes and smells, are held to be non-representational and are similarly subjective in perception, in the ways we explored in Chapter 1. However, for just these reasons, the expression of emotion in music is itself a deep and difficult philosophical problem and there is no agreement about how best to explain it.

Why, then, should the attribution of emotional properties to wine be any more doubtful or troublesome?

We might point first to the empirical fact, if it is a fact, that we readily attribute emotions to music, but not to wine. Is this a fact? I'm not at all certain that it is, or whether, if it is, it accurately reflects something inherent and necessary about the expressive potential of wine. As our previous discussion has shown, we do attribute all sorts of human characteristics to wine, including personal character traits that don't appear to be very far removed from emotional characteristics. If a wine can be cheerful or cheeky, brooding and pretentious, can it not also be happy? But even if the empirical claim is true, why should we think that it is anything more than a sociocultural or historically contingent matter, a matter of mere convention?

Perhaps if we began to appreciate wines in ways similar to those in which we appreciate art and music we could, or would, begin to see wines as expressive, in the "strong" sense of being capable of emotional expression. If we could not do this, however, then we would have reason to think that there is something about the nature of tastes and smells themselves in wine – and in our perceptual capacities – that bars them (but not sounds) from being capable of emotional expression as a matter of some sort of *physical necessity*. Is it somehow possible to imagine a culture that drank wine as expressing emotion, but failed to hear music as doing so?

Recall the thought that wine can be expressive only in virtue of association rather than because of intrinsic properties of its "content". We learn, say, to associate big fruity wines with hot climates and naturally call them sunny, cheerful, attractive or open, and it is by such trains of association that we come to employ the particular metaphors that we do, in the ways that we demonstrated in Chapter 2. This is not a rigidly mechanical process, but a creative and imaginative one, and yet, as we have seen, one that is governed by certain constraints and judgements about what "makes sense" of the perceptual object being described. This kind of association does not seem to be philosophically problematic, but the expression of emotion in abstract music does not seem reducible to this. So the question at issue is whether, even if we were to attribute emotion qualities to wines, these would really be explicable fully in terms of "mere" association and convention.

The only way to answer this is to examine some current philosophical theories of musical expression to see whether they entail anything about the impossibility of wine expressing emotion, and also whether music itself is legitimately ascribed emotion properties, and not merely in virtue of convention and association.

The central idea of what is sometimes known as the *contour theory* is that music resembles, in various ways, the outward expression of emotion by human beings. Steven Davies says: "The movement of music is *experienced* in the same way that bodily bearings or comportments indicative of a person's emotional states are … music is *experienced as dynamic*, as are human action and behaviour" (2006a: 151, emphasis added)

163

There are a couple of key features of this view relevant for our purposes. First, the role of intention is crucial. We hear music as expressive in virtue of the fact that "musical works and performances are designed to have most of their salient properties, including their emotion-resembling ones. So long as it is deliberately created, the appearance of emotion presented in the music is the result of an act of expression" (185). Second, and most importantly, Davies claims that "music is capable of expressing a fairly limited number of emotional types, but that it can express these objectively, so that suitable skilled and situated listeners agree highly in attributing them to music" (183).

The limited emotional types expressed are most plausibly identified, Davies argues, with those that have specific expressive behaviours associated with them and a rough and ready list of these have been compiled by empirical psychologists – sadness, happiness, anger, fear, surprise – the behavioural expressions of which all appear to have an evolutionary basis. Davies thus holds that expressiveness requires that there be:

> a wide coincidence in judgements of expressiveness by suitably qualified listeners under appropriate conditions. It is only with respect to broad categories of emotion – happiness versus sadness, for instance – that this consensus is achieved. (185)

The main alternative to this view is known as *hypothetical emotionalism* (or *persona theory*) and its point of departure is the concern that Davies's view cannot account for the capacity of music to express cognitively subtle and complex emotions such as hope, or "cheerful confidence turning to despair". Indeed, Davies explicitly denies that music can express any emotions more fine-grained than the broad types he points to. Davies's primary criticism of this view is that what the music supplies is simply too indefinite to sufficiently control our imaginings such that there will be sufficient agreement on what the music expresses.

To counter this, the hypothetical emotionalist argues that musical expression consists in imagining of the music that it presents a narrative or drama about a person who experiences the relevant emotions. That is, we attribute these emotions to an imagined persona in the music. To account for the agreement in and objectivity of our emotional attributions to music, such imaginings must be in some way constrained, but how? Jenefer Robinson, drawing on psychological research, claims that:

> the music's dynamic tension causes in the listener sensations or feelings of being pushed, prodded, pulled, dragged, and stirred. These primitive responses are largely noncognitive. They fuel and direct the narrative that listeners construct about the experience of the persona they hypothesize as residing in the music.
>
> (Quoted in Davies 2006b: 189)

Whatever explanation of musical expression one takes to be most plausible, however, one might think that it doesn't look promising for wine. First, wine – and the tastes and smells that constitute it – does not seem to have the right kind of resemblances to trigger the right kinds of expression-recognition responses in us. It doesn't appear, for example, to move through time or to have the "spatial" dimensions of pitch that sounds possess. It is the nature of musical movement, its passages of tension and relaxation, that allows or causes us to hear music as expressive, for it is the link to behaviour and comportment that resembles human emotional expression. For this reason it seems to be *naturally* the case that we hear music as emotional, even if the specific emotions heard in the music are culturally variable or layered with imaginative association. For this reason too it perhaps seems easier, more natural, to imagine a persona in music doing the expressing than it does in the case of wine. That is, imagining a persona in the wine would seem to be a purely contingent and idiosyncratic response. The non-expressive features of the wine do not seem to support such an activity.

Clearly, wine itself does not move, but our experience of very fine wines, and part of what we value in them, can be temporal. As our earlier discussion of the analogy between wine and music shows, we talk about "notes" in the wine coming into and going out of existence, blending with others, and involving certain transitions. Indeed these are some of the properties in virtue of which we *naturally* attribute expressive qualities to the wine.

It may be true that we don't naturally taste wine as resembling the bodily expressions of human emotion, given the absence of the right kind of movement. Yet, given the complexity of wine, and its ability to take on expressive characteristics partly in virtue of having been designed to do so, there seems to be no good reason for thinking that we could not in principle experience wines as expressing certain emotions and doing so not because of idiosyncratic imaginary associations but in virtue of intrinsic properties of the wine in combination with the right kinds of conventions.

The idea is this. Think of the manifold properties that we have already seen are used to ground the various conventions governing the application of metaphors to wine. These form part of the basis of the wine as an expressive vehicle. Now why could we not begin creating and appreciating wines as expressing more specific emotions? Instead of having a winemaker attempt to create a "subtle and sexy" wine, why could he not create one that was experienced as being happy, or sad? The key to doing so, I think, is whether it could make sense of our experience of a wine to so describe it: whether we could genuinely claim to understand the wine in virtue of attributing those properties to it. This may require in part the development of certain sophisticated conventions that serve to structure our understanding and appreciation of it, but it is not obvious that our ability to hear music as expressive does not also depend on there being in place the right kinds of conventions, background knowledge and cultural associations.

It is useful here to draw on a recent account of expressiveness given by Paul Noordhof that, on the one hand, offers what I contend is a more plausible account of musical expression than either of the two theories just examined, and on the other hand offers a general account of *expression* in terms of *expressiveness* that can be extended to encompass wine.

Noordhof argues that resemblance features are not *as such* part of the phenomenal content of our perceptual experience of expressive properties, nor are expressive properties experienced in terms of "as-if expression". Rather, we experience such properties *as expressive*, as properties with *expressive potential*, not as expressions *as of* some mental state.

> When we perceive expressive properties in a work of art, we imagine a particular kind of creative process which, when the expressive properties are those of emotions, is guided by emotions … we imagine how an emotion would be manifested through the creative process in non-expressively specified features of the artwork which realise the expressive property. (2008: 338)

That is, we imagine how some kind of creative process resulted in an object having just those features that we see as being expressive of that process. Those features might be the specific brush strokes on a canvas, the specific notes in a musical passage, or the specific tastes, smells and textures in a bottle of wine.

The main features of this account to note for our purpose are, first, that these features are experienced *as expressive* and not as being an *expression of*, and second that expressive perception (i.e. our perception of expressive properties) essentially involves the imagination. It is imaginative in so far as it is less "immediate" than normal perception, in which we simply passively see, for example, the properties of objects as belonging to them. Instead, it requires a certain engagement on our part, an engagement that adds something over and above the perception of the non-expressive features that constitute the expressive properties. That is, in the case of musical expression for example, it is possible (although it may at times be difficult) merely to hear noise, to hear the sounds as non-expressive. Similarly, in the case of wine, we can choose to focus just on the tastes and smells as tastes and smells, and not as bearing expressive or aesthetic properties. We have in principle some control over this, much like the control we have in classic cases of aspect or affordance perception, such as seeing the famous duck–rabbit figure as alternately either a duck, or a rabbit.

Now one advantage of this kind of account is that it is not limited to cases of emotional expression, but can explain the expressivity of ideas, attitudes or values. For example, we can see Mondrian's *Broadway Boogie Woogie* as expressive of jazz (or the feeling of listening to jazz) and can hear Debussy's *La Mer* as expressive of swirling movements of sea (or the experience of this).

As we witnessed in Chapter 4, perceiving the expressive character of artworks may require certain background knowledge concerning artistic intentions, art-historical styles, categories and genres and so on. As such, our experiences of expressive properties are cognitively penetrable. *La Mer* is expressive of the sea in virtue of the title of the piece and the intentions behind it; we perceive *Broadway Boogie Woogie* to be expressive of jazz given its relation to Mondrian's *oeuvre* specifically and the abstract expressionist style more generally. Much aesthetic experience – at least of artworks – is like this. What aesthetic properties a work seems to possess depends on the various categories against which the work is perceived, as we have seen.

Given that a creative process implies agency, expressive perception requires some kind of background "acceptance" or "awareness" – which might be more or less unconscious – of agency. When confronted with a known artefact, therefore, we approach it and appreciate and experience it with an implicit background belief in agency that allows us to see the features of the works as products of a creative process.

So, the thought is this. We perceive wine as expressive (through tasting it) partly in virtue of the fact that we are aware, even minimally, that it is an artefact created and designed to give rise to certain experiences in us, experiences that may involve the perception of expressive properties (if these are there to be perceived). Tastes and smells (and textures) can be skilfully combined and structured in wine to constitute, via interaction with us, certain expressive properties. These properties are response-dependent and not fully captured in non-expressive terms. Attributions of expressive properties to wine are thus the result of an imaginative awareness of agency guiding a process resulting in the specific non-expressive features (its tastes, smells, textures) partly constituting the expressive properties. What expressive properties a wine appears to us to have will depend on the range of factors that we have already examined, such as *terroir* and grape, the intentions of the winemaker, the knowledge and experience of the taster, and the category of appreciation against which it is judged, where these categories include those discussed in Chapter 4.

Of course, there may be some limits on expressiveness here. Perhaps there are far more natural, empirical – if not conventional – limits on the expressive potential of wine than of music. This would not be surprising and nor am I claiming otherwise. In so far as the objects of our different sense modalities can be compared, there is some sense to be made of the claim that music is *all in all* a more complicated experiential object, we can do more with it, it is more natural to hear it as expressive. It is, after all, more difficult to conceive what a wine would have to be like to be hopeful or sad.

Yet, like Davies, I think that there are limits too to what music can genuinely express. Indeed I myself am sceptical about the ability of abstract instrumental music *to be* hopeful, except in so far as we can imagine, if we wish, a persona in the music expressing hope. But if we do begin imagining expressive personas, it does not strike me that the expressive potential of wine or the objectivity of our judgements about such expression will *necessarily* suffer in comparison with music. In short, what counts as being "more natural" seems to me partly a question of degree, and the differences observed between wine and music entail nothing about the impossibility of experiencing wine as expressive of emotion.[4]

---

4. Indeed, it might be best to think of the experience of both musical and wine expression as *sui generis*; although it makes sense to use emotion terms to characterize such expressiveness, fundamentally the expression of, for instance, *terroir* and personality in wine cannot be fully specified other than by experiencing just those properties of the wine. Using emotion terms may be the best, but ultimately necessarily limited, way of trying to describe certain characteristics of objects like wine and music.

In any case, even if most wines are not generally experienced as expressive, the main issue is whether wine as such is *capable* of bearing expressive properties. Coupled with the right conventions and intentions it's not clear that anything intrinsic to tastes and smells precludes the possibility of emotional expression. An important convention in this context, for example, one that would affect the way in which wine can be experienced, could include encompassing fine wine under the umbrella concept of art, in the way suggested earlier in this chapter. Like complex artworks, it may be that the expressive properties of wine require expertise to perceive, and that only some wine will be capable of bearing some expressive properties. So long as the expressive properties attributed to wine are there to be experienced by the trained eye, however, that is enough to ensure expressivity. How automatic our expressive perception is will be subject to degree and relative to the level of expertise and background knowledge involved. As such, it is not impossible to imagine a culture drinking wine as expressing emotion, and perhaps even failing to hear music as doing so, even though it may be more or less generally true of our own actual culture that we more readily experience music as expressive than wine.

Conclusion

Truth, Beauty and Intoxication

I have endeavoured, throughout the course of this book, to show that wine can be an object of serious philosophical reflection and serious appreciative attention. I began, in Chapter 1, by rejecting sceptical claims – arising from common-sense intuitions, philosophical speculations and scientific study – about the inability of tastes and smells to provide us with genuine knowledge of objects. Such knowledge, in the case of wine, requires a certain level of training and expertise, and we saw that much of the empirical evidence frequently called on to undermine the existence of expertise actually instead supports it. It does so primarily in demonstrating that taste and smell perception is crucially affected and shaped by background knowledge and experience, and that this plays a key role in wine tasting.

We have seen that wine, as an object of appreciation, can be conceived as both an ordinary physical object consisting of perceptible chemical compounds in the external world, and as an imaginative, interpreted, experiential object that arises as a relation between us and this physical reality. In Chapter 2 we examined this connection between physical object and experience through the language used to describe and evaluate wine. We discovered that even some of the more extravagant flights of metaphorical fancy indulged by experts could be grounded in certain norms and conventions that established the relevant criteria of meaning and truth for wine judgements. Specifically, I argued that these norms and conventions, although in part themselves dependent on expertise, must ultimately be grounded in perceptible properties of the wine. Yet I also claimed that our judgements are essentially about our *experiences* of these properties, and it is ultimately these experiences that we hope to share with others when using appropriate metaphorical language. To the extent that we are successful we can have some claim to our judgements being objective.

Much of our energy has been expended in trying to pin down the objectivity of taste, and we have pursued it through the realms of chemicals and metaphors, of realism and relativism, of disagreements and expertise. Although ultimately rejecting a realist position on this issue, I have nonetheless attempted to defend the objectivity of wine tasting by articulating a notion of "understanding" that governs the appropriate appreciation of wine. I have explained this notion by exploring the nature and limits of metaphorical ascriptions; by articulating the role of categories in structuring our experiences and judgements of wine; by defending the existence and role of expertise; by outlining the role that imaginative reasoning plays in appropriate experience and judgement; and by listing values intrinsic to the nature of wine. By acknowledging a certain ineliminable relativism of taste, and a degree of fluidity within evaluative standards, categories and preferences, I have outlined a relativist position that I nonetheless think preserves a robust form of objectivity about our wine judgements and evaluations.

In doing this I hope to have diffused unjust charges of snobbery and undermined worries of elitism without in any way downplaying the obvious role that various factors extraneous to the intrinsic values of wine – economic, social, political – play, and have played, in its evaluation. I have refrained from saying very much about these complex issues, however, because they bear less on the philosophy of wine than they do on what we might call its sociology. And in any case, whatever the inflated gulf market forces might create between real quality and price, we can be sure that such quality is real, and we can hope that price more often than not reflects this.

Although my discussion has been motivated by the simple aim of showing that wine tasting is neither subjective nor arbitrary, a greater motivation has been the desire to highlight the crucial connection of objectivity to the appreciation of wine's rich and multifarious values. It is important to be objective, ultimately, because only in being so can one truly and fully recognize and experience these values. This kind of "aesthetic" or "evaluative" understanding of wine is thus a *sine qua non* of grasping a domain of appreciation that is intrinsically rewarding. As we noted in Chapter 5, one *ought* to try to notice the delicate balance of the Château Figeac, for otherwise one will have missed something of value that is there to be experienced. Moreover, achieving such understanding involves the cultivation and exercise of a range of cognitive, perceptual and imaginative capacities that are essential elements of the kinds of creatures we are, and the full development and deployment of which form an integral part of the nature of human flourishing. This is the issue I wish to dwell on for the remainder of this concluding chapter.

Among the valuable characteristics of wine, I highlighted – in addition to the sensory pleasures of particular odours, tastes and textures – balance, intensity, subtlety, complexity, being interesting or surprising, having personality and individuality, embodying *terroir*. I also noted the pleasures of discrimination, the satisfaction of interest, and the exercise of imaginative capacities. Among the chief values of wine, we have seen, are what might arguably be called aesthetic qualities: beauty, elegance and harmony, variety and unity, attractiveness, balance, delicacy, authenticity, refinement and subtlety, skilfulness, originality and uniqueness, and indeed any of the enormous panoply of evaluative aesthetic attributes that we denote in wine by the use of appropriate metaphors. The greatest wines will manifest these qualities to the highest degree, but even some less great wines will be capable of embodying some of these virtues to some degree.

Even such a limited list as this, I feel, goes a long way to justifying many of the claims I have made for the value of wine, yet without the ability to possess expressive qualities and to thereby acquire some sort of "meaning", the understanding we have attributed to wine tasting would remain, as it were, *sui generis* and without connection to issues of deep and lasting human concern and consequence. Hence my attempt to secure for wine some of the most important values possessed by artworks, by defending its expressive capabilities and comparing it in this respect to our appreciation of musical expression.

Allowing the arguments I offered to be moderately successful, however, there may yet be lingering doubts about the overall significance and value of wine in the life of beings such as ourselves. For still, one might claim, wine's actual, relatively limited capacity to embody certain intentions and express certain values and ideas (and perhaps even emotions) does not secure it an important place in the scheme of overall values. Relative to the finest compositions of the greatest composers, the finest works of the greatest writers, let alone relative to the indefinitely many other ways in which one can spend one's time, effort and hard-earned cash in benefiting the flourishing of human life, the appreciation of wine simply cannot, or should not, figure at all prominently. Indeed, in this light, it might be claimed to be perverse, frivolous and even immoral to hold otherwise.

It is tempting to reject such thoughts by dismissing the kinds of dubious comparisons that lie at their heart. Many of these appear to trade on implicit assumptions (a) that there is a clear hierarchy of aesthetic values established with reference to their bearing on deep and important human concerns, and (b) that in purported conflicts between aesthetic and moral values, the latter should always triumph. It is possible to reject both by pointing out that, mercifully, life is awash with a vast array of different values that fulfil different sorts of interests, needs and preferences. There is room for all of them in a full life, and the sheer multitude and variety is just an intrinsically good thing, like bio-diversity.

Moreover, many of these values are simply incommensurable and hence render vacuous or silly claims about the relative frivolity or triviality of the sensual pleasures induced by wine. Exiled to a desert island with a choice between Beethoven's late quartets and a case of Romanée-Conti for company, is it so obvious that the former would be, or ought to be, preferred? Is it really immoral to spend thousands of pounds on a case of Château Pétrus when that money could be given to some worthwhile charity? At the very least, any positive answer to these questions owes us a thorough account of the relation between different values and a powerful justification of the normative stance adopted.

Rather than succumb to this temptation, however, it is more worthwhile to explore a more positive and persuasive response to such qualms, one that stresses some of the important connections between the pleasures of wine and deep human concerns. This story affords us an account not merely of values that inanimate objects in the world can attain for human beings, but of how such values can enlighten us about ourselves.

Recall the idea proposed in Chapter 5 that through the expressive capacities of wine, and particularly in virtue of its expression of *terroir*, we can become aware, in some sense through tasting it, of a particular array of "life-values", of ideals and attitudes, and of traditions, customs, places and communities; of all those things that have allowed this wine to come to be made in just this way. This, I contend, is a kind of aesthetic understanding or awareness, yet it reflects values that are not just aesthetic, but also moral and cognitive. We learn about certain things that people have held dear, including the time and effort, seriousness and love involved in making an object that can cause intensely pleasurable experiences in others; experiences, moreover, that can be shared. These qualities, in turn, reflect a particular type of – and view of – civilized life and the cultivation of distinctly human virtues and values. Wine, even relatively simple wine, can embody and convey these in a unique way, of which other foods and beverages are at least much less capable, and which cannot be similarly achieved by other art forms. For wine is essentially a living and evolving thing, and each bottle has its own particular past and future that can be tasted in it.

It is in these ways that wine displays its particular virtues of truth, beauty and intoxication. Why *in vino veritas*? Because the intoxication wine brings loosens the tongue, opens the mind, and weakens the resolve of sobriety, which normally controls and hampers the truth from escaping one's lips. As poets and philosophers since Plato have noted, this gives wine an especially elevated status as the paradigmatic social lubricant, facilitating and enhancing those fundamentally moral virtues of sociability, conversation, sincerity, humour and graciousness. Indeed even so otherwise austere a philosopher as Immanuel Kant preached such virtues, hailing wine as a necessary component of the perfect dinner party and allowing that, under its sway, the threshold of sobriety could be crossed for moral reasons (see Cohen 2008). Rather than wine's intoxicating quality distancing one from the world, therefore, as do other drugs and alcoholic beverages, it instead engages us in, and makes us more receptive to, important and authentic ways of experiencing ourselves and sharing those experiences with others. It enables and deepens the *sensus communis*.[1]

There is thus a kind of truthfulness in the intoxicating experiences that great wine provides, and there is also a deep kind of beauty. The unity in variety, the harmony and sensuality, the expression of *terroir*, the complexity and finesse, the balanced and patterned tastes, smells and textures in wine, the skilful achievement the wine represents, are also parts of the aesthetic experience of drinking wine, the very parts of which its beauty is constituted. But beauty is not merely a sensory phenomenon, for it can have a cognitive function, as mathematicians have long suspected. Through perceiving this beauty we learn about the human values, ideals and ways of life that we have been discussing. We learn that the sensory pleasures enjoyed by the body can be subjected to a high level of artistic creativity, and can be elevated into an object of intellectual attention and appreciation. We learn more about our multifarious interests and pleasures, the nature of appreciation, and the meaningfulness and emotional expressivity that objects in the world can attain for us. And we become aware of our own powerful and subtle capacities for discriminating and evaluating.

In learning all of this we are also cultivating and exercising the cognitive, perceptual and imaginative capacities that are central to our flourishing as human beings. In understanding and appreciating wine, therefore, we thereby come to better understand and

---

1. See Scruton (2009: ch. 5) for a fuller discussion of these issues.

appreciate ourselves, and to taste the unity of truth, beauty and the good (life).

Of course these observations, despite being hallowed by tradition, may be difficult or impossible to prove, and they are perhaps at least as much a matter for empirical study as philosophical reflection. Moreover, as I noted right at the outset, the nature of such experiences cannot be adequately reported or captured in words, any more than great works of music or art can be so captured. One needs to drink for oneself; and the better the wine, the better your chances of tasting the truth of these observations. Indeed there is no better, or more pleasurable, way of combining philosophical reflection with empirical study.

Bibliography

Allhof, F. (ed.) 2008. *Wine and Philosophy: A Symposium on Thinking and Drinking*. Oxford: Blackwell.

Ashenfelter, O., R. E. Quandt & G. M. Taber 2008. "Wine-Tasting Epiphany: An Analysis of the 1976 California vs. France Tasting". See Allhof (2008), 237–47.

Bach, K. 2007. "Knowledge, Wine and Taste: What Good is Knowledge (in Enjoying Wine)?" See Smith (2007a), 21–40.

Bach, K. 2008. "Talk about Wine?" See Allhof (2008), 95–110.

Beckett, N. 2008. *1001 Wines You Must Try Before You Die*. London: Cassell.

Bender, J. 2001. "Sensitivity, Sensibility, and Aesthetic Realism". *Journal of Aesthetics and Art Criticism* **59**: 73–83.

Bender, J. 2008. "What the Wine Critic Tells Us". See Allhof (2008), 125–36.

Budd, M. 1995. *Values of Art: Pictures, Poetry and Music*. Harmondsworth: Penguin.

Budd, M. 2002. *The Aesthetic Appreciation of Nature: Essays on the Aesthetics of Nature*. Oxford: Clarendon Press.

Burnham, D. & O. M. Skilleas 2008. "You'll Never Drink Alone: Wine Tasting and Aesthetic Practice". See Allhof (2008), 157–71.

Charters, S. 2008. "Listening to the Wine Consumer: The Art of Drinking". See Allhof (2008), 186–202.

Charters, S. 2007. "On the Evaluation of Wine Quality". See Smith (2007a), 157–82.

Cohen, A. 2008. "The Ultimate Kantian Experience: Kant on Dinner Parties". *History of Philosophy Quarterly* **25**: 315–36.

Crane, T. 2007. "Wine as an Aesthetic Object". See Smith (2007a), 141–56.

Davies, S. 1997. "Contra the Hypothetical Persona in Music". In *Emotion and the Arts*, M. Hjort & S. Laver (eds), 95–109. Oxford: Oxford University Press.

Davies, S. 2006a. *The Philosophy of Art*. Oxford: Blackwell.

Davies, S. 2006b. "Artistic Expression and the Hard Case of Pure Music". In *Contemporary Debates in Aesthetics and the Philosophy of Art*, M. Kieran (ed.), 179–91. Oxford: Blackwell.

Deroy, O. 2007. "The Power of Tastes: Reconciling Science and Subjectivity". See Smith (2007a), 99–126.

Dilworth, J. 2008. "Mmmmm … not Aha! Imaginative vs. Analytical Experiences of Wines". See Allhof (2008), 81–94.

Gale, G. 2008. "Who Cares If You Like It, This Is a Good Wine Regardless". See Allhof (2008), 172–85.

Goode, J. 2005. *The Science of Wine: From Vine to Glass*. Los Angeles, CA: University of California Press.

Goode, J. 2007. "Wine and the Brain". See Smith (2007a), 79–98.

Goode, J. 2008. "Experiencing Wine: Why Critics Mess Up (Some of the Time)". See Allhof (2008), 137–54.

Grahm, R. 2008. "The Soul of Wine: Digging for Meaning". See Allhof (2008), 219–24.

Hume, D. 1987. *Essays: Moral, Political, and Literary*. London: Liberty Fund.

Jefford, A. & P. Draper 2007. "The Art and Craft of Wine". See Smith (2007a), 199–218.

Johnson, H. 2002. *The Story of Wine*. London: Octopus.

Korsmeyer, C. 2008. "The Meaning of Taste and the Taste of Meaning". In *Arguing About Art: Contemporary Philosophical Debates*, A. Neill & A. Ridley (eds), 30–52. London: Routledge.

Kramer, M. 2008. "The Notion of Terroir". See Allhof (2008), 225–34.

Lehrer, A. 2007. "Can Wines Be Brawny?: Reflections on Wine Vocabulary". See Smith (2007a), 127–40.

Lehrer, A. 2009. *Wine and Conversation*. Oxford: Oxford University Press.

Lehrer, K. & A. Lehrer 2008. "Winespeak or Critical Communication? Why People Talk about Wine". See Allhof (2008), 111–22.

Levinson, J. 2006. "Musical Expressiveness as Hearability-as-Expression". In *Contemporary Debates in Aesthetics and the Philosophy of Art*, M. Kieran (ed.), 192–204. Oxford: Blackwell.

Lycan, W. G. 2000. "The Slighting of Smell (with a Brief Word on the Slighting of Chemistry)". In *Of Minds and Molecules: New Philosophical Perspectives on Chemistry*, N. Bhushan & S. Rosenfeld (eds), 273–89. Oxford: Oxford University Press.

Noordhof, P. 2008. "Expressive Perception as Projective Imagining". *Mind and Language* **23**: 329–58.

Origgi, G. 2007. "Wine Epistemology: The Role of Reputational and Ranking Systems in the World of Wine". See Smith (2007a), 183–98.

Peynaud, É. 1987. *The Taste of Wine: The Art and Science of Wine Appreciation*. San Francisco: Wine Appreciation Guild.

Robinson, Jancis (ed.) 1999. *The Oxford Companion to Wine*. Oxford: Oxford University Press.

Robinson, Jancis 2003. *Jancis Robinson's Wine Course*. London: Ted Smart.

Robinson, Jenefer 1998. "The Expression and Arousal of Emotion in Music". In *Musical Worlds: New Directions in the Philosophy of Music*, P. Alperson (ed.), 13–22. University Park, PA: Penn State University Press.

Scruton, R. 2007. "The Philosophy of Wine". See Smith (2007a), 1–20.

Scruton, R. 2009. *I Drink Therefore I Am: A Philosopher's Guide to Wine*. London: Continuum.

Sibley, F. 2001. "Tastes, Smells, and Aesthetics". In *Approach to Aesthetics: Collected Papers on Philosophical Aesthetics*, J. Benson, B. Redfern & J. Roxbee Cox (eds), 207–55. Oxford: Clarendon Press.

Smith, B. (ed.) 2007a. *Questions of Taste: The Philosophy of Wine*. Oxford: Signal Books.

Smith, B. 2007b. "The Objectivity of Tastes and Tasting". See Smith (2007a), 41–78.

Sweeney, K. 2008. "Is There Coffee or Blackberry in My Wine?". See Allhof (2008), 205–218.

Telfer, E. 2008. "Food as Art". In *Arguing About Art: Contemporary Philosophical Debates*, A. Neill & A. Ridley (eds), 11–29. London: Routledge.

Walton, K. 1970. "Categories of Art". *Philosophical Review* **79**: 334–67.

Weinberg, J. 2008. "Taste How Expensive This Is: A Problem of Wine and Rationality". See Allhof (2008), 257–74.

Winiarski, W. 2008. "The Old World and the New: Worlds Apart?" See Allhof (2008), 248–56.

Index